John Brett: a Pre-Raphaelite on the Shores of Wales

Tourist Map
OF
NORTH & SOUTH WALES
WITH ADJOINING PORTION OF
ENGLAND
From the Ordnance Survey.

Published by Catherall & Prichard, Eastgate St. Row,
CHESTER.

RAILWAYS SHEWN THUS

British Miles

John Brett: a Pre-Raphaelite on the Shores of Wales

National Museum & Gallery Cardiff
2001

First published in Great Britain in 2001 by the National Museums & Galleries of Wales, Cathays Park, Cardiff, CF10 3NP

On the occasion of the exhibition
John Brett: a Pre-Raphaelite on the Shores of Wales
National Museum & Gallery Cardiff
14 August - 25 November 2001

ISBN 0 7200 0507 8
(Welsh version: 0 7200 0508 6)

British Library Cataloguing-in-Publication Data
A catalogue record for this book is available from the British Library

Design and production by Arwel Hughes and Mari Gordon
Printed in Wales by Hackman Print

Cover: *Fishguard Bay,* 1883, Collection Mr & Mrs Alfred M. Rankin, Jr

Frontispiece: John Hicklin, *The Illustrated Hand-book of North Wales*, c. 1850

Photos are credited by kind permission of the owners, and to the following:
Aberdeen Art Gallery and Museums (cats 3, 33)
Ashmolean Museum, Oxford (Newall, fig. 1)
Birmingham Museums & Art Gallery (cat. 13)
Board of Trustees of the National Museums and Galleries on Merseyside
(Walker Art Gallery, Liverpool) (Newall, fig. 3)
Bridgeman Art Library (Newall, figs 4, 5)
British Museum (Newall, fig. 10)
Christie's (cats 20, 35)
Cleveland Museum of Art (cats 19, 26)
The Forbes Magazine Collection, New York (cat. 36)
G.ten Photography, University of Manchester (cat. 17)
Stephen Hopkinson, John Whybrow Ltd (cat. 7)
Indianapolis Museum of Art, James E. Roberts Fund (Newall, fig. 8)
Nicholas Moss, Rodney Todd-White & Son (cats 1, 2, 6, 9, 12, 14, 21, 22, 24, 27, 29, 30, 34,
Cordingly, figs 6, 10)
National Maritime Museum (cat. 5, Cordingly, fig. 11)
National Museums & Galleries of Wales (cats 8, 10, 11, 15, 25, 28, Cordingly, figs 2, 5,
Sumner, figs 2, 4)
Pembrokeshire Record Office / David Perkins, Castle Photography (Sumner, fig.3)
Phillips Auctioneers (cat. 16)
James Phillips (cat. 4, Cordingly, figs 4, 7)
Sotheby's (cat. 37, Cordingly, fig. 9)
Sunderland Museum & Winter Gardens, Tyne & Wear Museums (cat. 31)
© Tate, London, 2001 (cat. 18, Newall, figs 2, 6, 7)
John Webb (Newall, fig. 2)
Williamson Art Gallery & Museum, Birkenhead, Wirral (cat. 32)

Contents

Exhibition Committee and Authors

David Cordingly

Christopher Gridley (researcher)

Kate Lowry

Christopher Newall

Ann Sumner (editor)

Director's Preface

'John Brett: a Pre-Raphaelite on the Shores of Wales' is an exhibition of seascapes of the coasts of Wales. It forms part of a programme that celebrates the influence of the land and subject matter of Wales on visual artists, past and present. It also, I believe, achieves a goal to which all good exhibitions should aspire – it transforms our understanding by original, groundbreaking research. John Brett has been seen as a promising Victorian painter, whose career faltered in the mid-1860s, and whose later seascapes were deemed repetitious. Equally Wales, outside Snowdonia and the artists' colony of the Conwy valley, is thought to have had little to offer the later nineteenth-century artist. Many of the works in this exhibition prove otherwise and some are seen by the public for the first time since the artist himself exhibited them. We also learn much about Brett's professional practice, how he worked, the materials and methods he used, and the changing market for his paintings.

This is the first exhibition to look specifically at Brett's later career, after his association with Ruskin had ended, and the first to be devoted exclusively to him since 1893. It provides a very different insight into an artist whose reputation has previously rested, almost entirely, upon his early Pre-Raphaelite works. It reveals not only his talents as a sea-painter, his love of ships, and attachment to the coast of Wales, but also, in his charming photographs, his deep affection for his family. The family's idyllic holidays in Wales were spent swimming, sailing, fishing and walking the coastal paths, while their father sketched and painted. The paintings themselves depict a vanished world before the advent of mass-tourism, when the coasts were thronged with working sailing ships.

The National Museum & Gallery, though exceptionally rich in nineteenth-century French painting and sculpture from the 1840s onwards, has less extensive collections of British art of this period. This is reflected in our temporary exhibition programme, as the last exhibition on a Victorian artist curated here was 'Arthur Hughes', back in 1971. A 'John Brett in Wales' exhibition was first suggested by Christopher Gridley, a connoisseur of Victorian painting and a long-standing friend of the National Museums & Galleries of Wales. It is largely the result of his energy, support and unfailing enthusiasm that this project has come to fruition. We have also benefited greatly from the scholarship of David Cordingly, formerly Keeper of Pictures at the National Maritime Museum and the art historian Christopher Newall. Both have contributed essays to this catalogue. The exhibition was curated by Ann Sumner, who joined us as Curator (Fine Art) in 2000, with a wealth of experience of pre-twentieth-century British art. We are deeply grateful to all four of them who have worked as a Committee for this past year. Our thanks are particularly extended to Christopher Gridley, for whom this has been a labour of love. Exhibitions are the result of teamwork, and I should also mention Kate Lowry, who writes here on John Brett's working methods, Helen Waters, Tim Egan, Angela Gaffney, Christine MacKay, Beth McIntyre, Lyn Jarman Davies, Oliver Fairclough and their colleagues in the Department of Art. The National Museums & Galleries of Wales are a unique resource of knowledge about the landscape and history of Wales, and Richard Bevins (Department of Geology), David Jenkins (Department of Industry), Eleri Evans (Education) and John Kenyon (Library) have all provided much vital information and advice. Many works are reproduced from new transparencies made by our Photography Department, and the catalogue was designed and produced by Arwel Hughes.

Outside the National Museums & Galleries of Wales, the following individuals have given of their time and expertise to assist with the research and planning of this exhibition and to them all we are extremely grateful; Jon Astbury (Tate Britain), David Barrie (NACF), Nicholas Bagshawe, Judith Bronkhurst (Witt Library), Michael

Brookstone (Julian Simon Fine Art Ltd), Peter Brown (Christie's), Diana Browning, Johnny Bull, Catherine Clement (Tate Britain), Philip Davies, Wayne Debeugny (Ordnance Survey, Southampton), Duke's of Dorchester, Philip Eastwood (Williamson Art Gallery and Museum), Simon Edsor (Fine Art Society), Laurence Ehlers (Phillips), John Evans, Jane Farrington (Birmingham Museums and Art Gallery), Jocelyn Feilding (Jocelyn Feilding Fine Art Ltd), Olga Ferguson (Aberdeen City Art Gallery), James Gadd (Sotheby's Billingshurst), Michael Gibbs (Swansea Museum), Catherine Gordon (Witt Library), Peter Goodridge, Gavin Graham (Gavin Graham Gallery), Jane Hamilton (Agnews), Julian Hartnoll, Robert Hastie, Michael Hickox, Jane Holmes (National Maritime Museum), Stephen Hopkinson (John Whybrow Ltd), Juliet Horsley (Sunderland Museum and Winter Gardens), Arthur Jaynes (National Maritime Museum), Mark Jerram (Jerram Gallery), George Kidner, Marie Lewis (Pembrokeshire Record Office), Robin Llywelyn (Portmerion Village), Annabel Macrae (Forbes Magazine Collection, New York), Rupert Maas (Maas Gallery), Jennifer Melville (Aberdeen City Art Gallery), Judith Methuen Campbell, Paul Mitchell (Paul Mitchell Ltd), Nicholas Moss (Rodney Todd-White & Son), Peter Nahum (Leicester Galleries), Gabriel Norton (Agnews), Sally Oliver, Charles Omell (Omell Galleries), Guy Peppiatt (Sotheby's), James Phillips, Roger Quarm (National Maritime Museum), Peter Roberts (Cardigan Heritage Centre), Michael Pollard (G.ten Photography, University of Manchester), Japonica Sheridan (Christie's, South Kensington), Colin Simpson (Williamson Art Gallery and Museum), Janet Small (National Maritime Museum), Elizabeth Smallwood (Birmingham Museums and Art Gallery), Claire Smith (Christie's), Allen Staley, Lord Stanley of Alderney, Colin Starkey (National Maritime Museum), Simon Taylor (Sotheby's), Anita Thomas (Pembrokeshire County Library), Derek Trillo (G.ten Photography, University of Manchester), Ian Warrell (Tate Britain), Ken Williams (Fishguard and District Historical Society), Andrew Wilton (Tate Britain), Christopher Wood.

I would like to express my particular thanks to Robert Tear, Martin Beisley (Christie's), Michael Day (Burlington Paintings), Anthony Richards (Pembrokeshire Coast National Park), Ann Hughes (Fishguard Historical Society), Henrietta Pattinson (Sotheby's), Sian Jones (National Trust, Gower). Charles Brett, Martin Brett, Mary Horsfield, Pip Smith and Peter Watson, all descendants of the artist, have greatly assisted with research. The exhibition was made possible by the kindness and generosity of the lenders, who are listed on p. 121. They include many private owners, some of whom prefer to remain anonymous and all of whom have been tremendously supportive.

The exhibition was generously sponsored by Phillips Auctioneers, where I must pay an especial tribute to Antonia Hawke, Victoria Millward and Sophie Money and thank them for their support and keen interest in this enterprise. Our thanks are also extended to the Friends of the National Museum & Gallery for their kind sponsorship of this publication. It is hoped that the stimulus of this small but choice exhibition will encourage further research into Brett's later career and his association with other areas in the United Kingdom that inspired him such as Cornwall and Scotland.

Anna Southall

Director, National Museums & Galleries of Wales

Chronology

1831	John Brett is born on 8 December at Bletchingley, Surrey
1846	Brett's father is permanently stationed at the Cavalry Depot, Maidstone
1852	Brett reads John Ruskin's pamphlet on *Pre-Raphaelitism*
1853	Admitted as a student to the Royal Academy Schools
1856	Exhibits for the first time at the Royal Academy. Spends the summer in Switzerland, works on *The Glacier of Rosenlaui*
1858	*The Stonebreaker* is exhibited at the Royal Academy. In June he travels to Val d'Aosta in the Italian Alps
1859	*Val d'Aosta* is exhibited at the RA
1861	Sketching tour in vicinity of Lake Geneva. Winters in Florence
1863	Sails on steamship *Scotia* from Dover to Bay of Naples. Winters in Capri
1865	In Capri with Georgina Weldon. Visits Isle of Wight
1866	First recorded visit to Wales, at age of 35. Stays on Anglesey with Georgina Weldon
1867	Exhibits his first seascape inspired by the Anglesey visit at the RA entitled *Lat. 53⁰ 15' N, Long 5⁰ 10' W* (location unknown). Voyage on the yacht *Victoria* from Portsmouth to the Firth of Clyde. Winters on Anglesey again
1869/70	Meets Mary Howcroft who comes to live with him as his wife
1871	Visits Wales again with their baby, Michael, born that year, the first of seven children. They visit north Pembrokeshire and Snowdonia. Brett is elected a Fellow of the Royal Astronomical Society
1875	Spends the summer and early autumn in north Wales with three of their children Michael 4, Daisy 2½ and Jasper 9 months old
1879	Spends three months on the coast near Tenby, staying at Penally; begins writing their *Early Travels of our Children* in September at Penally
1880	*Britannia's Realm* is exhibited at the Royal Academy and purchased for the Chantrey Bequest
1881	Elected an Associate of the Royal Academy
1882	Brett makes a reconnaissance visit to Fishguard in April and returns with the family to spend the summer and early autumn at Newport in north Pembrokeshire
1883	Brett purchases the schooner *Viking* and the Brett family with the 13 man crew make a voyage in her around the British Isles. During late July they sail along the Pembrokeshire coastline, from Milford Haven around St David's Head, past Fishguard to Cardigan and anchor at Holyhead
1884	Brett family cruise in the *Viking* from Portsmouth to Cherbourg and Guernsey
1886	*Three Months on the Scottish Coast* exhibition is held by Brett at the Fine Art Society, London. Brett finally negotiates to purchase Windy Hall Farm in Fishguard
1887	Brett family spend summer on the Gower peninsula. On return to London in October Brett organises an exhibition *Four Months on the Gower Coast 1887* held at his Harley Street studio
1888	*The Earth's Shadow on the Sky* is exhibited at the Royal Academy. Work begins on the building of Brett's house, 'Daisyfield' in Putney
1891	*The Isles of Skomer and Skokham* based on a sketch of 1883 is exhibited at the Royal Academy. The Brett family spend the summer at the village of Aberporth, near Cardigan
1892	Brett leaves his studio in Harley Street and henceforth works at home in Putney. *Pearly Summer* is exhibited at the Royal Academy
1896	Travels to France to see *Isles of the Sirens* hung at the Paris Salon. Brett sells Windy Hall Farm, Fishguard
1902	January 7. Dies at his Putney home, aged 70

Abbreviations

AJ

Art Journal

Book of Pictures

John Brett, 'Book of Pictures being a record of the size, subject Price and destination of my principal productions From this year 1879'

Brett, *Three Months on the Scottish Coast*

John Brett, 'The Commentaries', *Three Months on the Scottish Coast – A Series of Sketches and Pictures painted during the summer of the present year*, exhibition catalogue, Fine Art Society, London, 1886

Cordingly

David Cordingly, 'The Life of John Brett – Painter of Pre-Raphaelite Landscapes and Seascapes', PhD thesis, University of Sussex, 1983

Early Travels

'Memoranda of the Early travels of our children written for them by John Brett and Mary Brett on alternate Sundays commencing in the Autumn of 1879 at Penally'

Marsh, *Christina Rossetti*

Jan Marsh, *Christina Rossetti – A Literary Biography*, London, 1994

Lewis, *Pondered Vision*

David Alan Lewis, 'Pondered Vision: The Art and Life of John Brett, A.R.A., 1830 – 1902', PhD thesis, University Graduate School Henry Redford Hope School of Fine Arts, Indiana University, 1995.

Newall, *Inchbold*

Christopher Newall, *John William Inchbold – Pre-Raphaelite Landscape Artist*, exhibition catalogue,   Leeds City Art Gallery, 1993

Potter, *Journal*

Beatrix Potter, *Journal*, transcribed from her writings by Leslie Linder, London, 1966

Ruskin, *Works*

E.T. Cook and Alexander Wedderburn (eds), *The Works of John Ruskin*, thirty-nine volumes, London, 1903 –12

Staley, *Pre-Raphaelite Landscape*

Allen Staley, *The Pre-Raphaelite Landscape*, Oxford, 1973 (chapter X 'John Brett', pp.124-37)

Brett's *Studio Log book*

Studio Logbook 1887 – 98, Studio Logbook 1894 – 1901

Wilcox and Newall

Scott Wilcox and Christopher Newall, *Victorian Landscape Watercolors*, exhibition catalogue, Yale Center for British Art, New Haven, Connecticut, 1992

Introduction

John Brett is best known as the Pre-Raphaelite artist who produced such familiar paintings as *The Stonebreaker* of 1858 (illustrated p.18) and *Val d'Aosta* of 1859 (illustrated p.19), with their truthfulness to nature and meticulous attention to detail. He was an associate in the mid-1850s of Millais and Holman Hunt, both of whom were influential upon his artistic development. He was also a friend for some years of D.G. Rossetti. In 1852 Brett read the Victorian art critic John Ruskin's pamphlet *Pre-Raphaelitism*. In the November of that year he absorbed *The Stones of Venice* but it was the fourth volume of *Modern Painters*, published in 1856, which concentrated upon the representation of mountain scenery, that had the greatest impact upon the artist. In 1858 Ruskin praised *The Stonebreaker* in his *Academy Notes* and apparently played a role in encouraging Brett to return to the Alps again. This visit led to the painting of *Val d'Aosta*, eventually acquired by Ruskin. During the mid-1860s Brett sailed to the Mediterranean and drew inspiration from the coastline around Capri and Sorrento. Brett had always loved the sea and was a keen sailor, purchasing his own boat on his return to England in 1865. He shared this passion with his youngest brother Edwin (cat. 2).

Brett turned increasingly to the sea for inspiration during this period and began experimenting with pure marine subjects, although sadly all the early works of this type are now lost or unlocated. A decade later he had devised the type of sea view where no indication is given of the painter's vantage-point, as in for example, *The British Channel from the Dorset Cliffs*, Tate, London (1871). He began to make regular summer explorations of the British coast and Devon, Cornwall, the Channel Islands, Scotland and especially Wales became favourite haunts. He was, by this time, devoting his career to painting pure marine or coastal scenes, usually with a negligible human element (cats 15 & 36 are the only paintings in the current exhibition to include figures), which were regularly exhibited at the Royal Academy and well reviewed. His only

Fig. 1, *Self Portrait*, 1883, Aberdeen Art Gallery and Museums (cat. 3)

rival in the painting of seascapes was his contemporary and friend Henry Moore (1831 – 1895), the principal sea-painter of the day. Initially Brett's paintings were in great demand, from private collectors such as the Birmingham manufacturer William Kenrick and later loyal patrons like the Scottish physician Dr James Watt Black, as well as from newly established museums. This was fortunate since he had by the l870s a rapidly expanding young family to support. In the early 1880s he enjoyed great success and was able to purchase his own schooner the *Viking*, build a new home in London and purchase property in

Fishguard with the intention of building a summer holiday home there. By the early 1890s the market for his seascapes had sadly diminished and he experienced severe financial problems. Relations between Ruskin and Brett had gradually broken down in the early 1860s; nonetheless Ruskin gave a guarded approval of Brett's change of style and subject matter. In response to a Channel Island subject on display at the 1875 Royal Academy he wrote, 'Mr Brett, in his coast scenes . . . gives us things, without thoughts; and the fuliginous moralists . . . thoughts – such as they are – without things: by all means let us rather have the geographical synopsis'.[1] Elsewhere Brett's seascapes were wholeheartedly acclaimed. In 1880, one of his finest Welsh seascapes, *Britannia's Realm* (cat. 18), a breathtaking view of calm sea off Tenby with a selection of sailing vessels, was one of the sensations of the Royal Academy summer exhibition. It was purchased for the nation by the Chantrey Bequest for £600. This was perhaps the zenith of Brett's career in terms of public esteem, and was followed by his election as an Associate Academician the subsequent year.

The present exhibition compares and contrasts some of his larger paintings like *Britannia's Realm* (cat. 18), *The Isles of Skomer and Skokham* (cat. 33) and *Earth's Shadow on the Sky* (cat. 31) from public collections, with smaller paintings and sketches of Welsh scenes which are less well known. These latter works have generally remained in private collections and many have never been previously exhibited. Both sketches and larger finished paintings were intended for display and were thus framed and offered for sale. The paintings were generally sold at the Academy exhibitions and provincial exhibitions such as those in Manchester and Birmingham, while the sketches were often sold through his Harley Street studio. Brett had a close working relationship with one particular framer, R. Dolman and Son. His seascapes, whether sketches or finished paintings, are often fitted into a distinctive Dolman design frame. The desirability of the sketches for his patrons is established by Brett's observation in October 1879, that 'within the last half dozen years or so the sale of oil sketches has comprised the chief part in number of (his) commercial transactions'.[2] He noted that none of these sketches was ever signed but they were always dated and mostly inscribed with the location. Larger paintings and all those exhibited at the Royal Academy were always signed. The sketches were painted on standard size canvases as 'a matter of convenience', he explained, because of the 'difficulties of porterage and

steadiness in a wind'.[3] For Brett such a sketch should amount to 'a single observation unadulterated, comprising whatever happens to occur at the time, and as much of it as circumstances allow to be recorded at one sitting'.[4] By contrast, it was his view that a 'finished picture is deliberately done under favourable conditions of light and shelter and is generally an abstract of several observations supplemented by whatever is deemed favourable to the presentation of the subject'.[5]

Brett used mathematical theory to determine the size of his canvases, selecting a shape that is two equal squares side by side. He believed that the eye 'can include easily an azimuth of sixty degrees, but all paintable phenomena in nature occur within an angle of about fifteen degrees above or below the horizon. All the clouds above the altitude are diffuse'.[6] He therefore excludes the sky above and the foreground below the thirty-degree range.

The careful observation of weather conditions and geological formations was key to the success of Brett's seascapes and coastal subjects. 'Sentiment in landscape' he once noted, 'is chiefly dependent on meteorology . . . without the command of the heavens the landscape-painter could produce only diagrams', adding that when the 'habits of the clouds are known there is no occasion for experiments in effect.'[7] He often made careful observations of clouds and geological features in his sketchbooks, with inscribed annotations to jog his memory when he was working back in his London studio. His keen eye for detail is illustrated for instance in such passages as this written in 1879 after a sketching expedition in a boat off Monkstone Point, near Tenby: 'cliffs (that) are very varied and beautifully contorted bed of (I suppose) limestone of darkish grey often stained with iron orange, black in the spray, and yellowish brown, rough and barnacled to the water's edge, touched here and there with vegetation towards the fields at top, and with bushy cover in the ravines'.[8] His detailed knowledge of boats and shipping is also reflected in his accurate depictions of vessels and their rigging, but he was less interested in ornithology. Some of his sea birds are positioned in inappropriate surroundings such as kittiwakes feeding on sandbanks or cormorants shown on beaches when they would be most likely to be situated on cliff tops.

Fig. 2, *Newport Castle 10 Sep. 1882*, original photograph, Collection Granddaughter of the artist

Brett's work as a pioneering photographer is also highlighted in this exhibition. A number of his beautiful original pictures of his wife Mary, and of their children, often taken while on holiday in Wales, as well as images of the *Viking*, are included. Some were mounted with his inscriptions, and as such, provide vivid accounts of the relaxed and informal life that Brett and his family led together. During their summer sojourns by the sea, Sundays were generally set aside for photography. On 5 October 1879 Brett wrote from Penally: 'I have been rather busy with the camera. Have got some views of the harbour of Tenby and several lovely groups of the kids in the garden'.[9]

This exhibition establishes Brett's particular passion for the landscape and coastline of Wales and in the course of forty years from the late l860s onwards he produced as many as two hundred Welsh views. Initially he visited Anglesey and Snowdonia, areas much frequented by artists since the late eighteenth century. Brett and his young family also spent that idyllic summer of l879 at Penally, near Tenby, a town which had long been established as a fashionable seaside resort. However, it was the isolated coastline of north Pembrokeshire around Fishguard and Newport that Brett most admired. They had first visited the area in

1871 and Brett was soon struck by the artistic possibilities of the more remote stretches of that coastline, painting such dramatic and yet inaccessible inlets as Aberfforest (*Forest Cove*, cat. 25). Newport was gradually becoming a tourist destination during the latter part of the nineteenth century. However both Fishguard and Newport remained little visited until the development of the harbour in the 1890s. In 1882 it took the family two days to travel from London to Fishguard, by rail and then by horse-drawn bus. The return journey at the close of the summer, was equally tiring according to Brett, it being 'the most dreary train journey, the train stopping at every station'.[10]

Yet it was the town of Fishguard and the surrounding area which Brett loved best. Not only did it have 'very considerable resources in the way of beauty' but it was also 'well adapted for boating exploits.'[11] Writing to

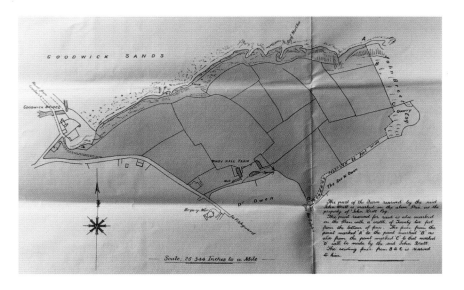

Fig. 3, *Map of Windy Hall Farm*, Pembrokeshire Record Office, ref. D/WW/55/8

his brother Arthur, many years later, Brett gave a summary of the parts of the coastline of the British Isles that he knew well and admired. The survey ended with a description of the coast near Fishguard and specifically of the parcel of land called Windy Hall Farm which he still owned there: 'There is in short only one really satisfactory seaside place on the whole British coast. It is an extremely beautiful promontory cut off from the world by a high road at its base . . . there is a little port to the east of it and a mile of sand on the west flank. There are lovely mountains and trout streams. The promontory measures 47 acres. It is my own property, but I am grieved to say I shall now have to sell it. I bought the freehold about a dozen years ago hoping some day to build on it for a colony of friends and a summer house for ourselves but alas there is a board up now 'This estate to be sold".[12]

fascination with boats and the sea with his devotion to family life. This is the first exhibition to be devoted to Brett's work since his death and as it concentrates upon his later career it reveals his talent as a marine artist and a painter of coastal areas. It especially focuses attention upon his particular attachment to Wales and its varied shoreline.

Ann Sumner
Curator (Fine Art)

Fig. 4, *Children Swimming in the Sea*, original photograph,
Collection Peter Watson, great-grandson of the artist

[1] Ruskin, *Works*, vol. XIV p.297.
[2] *Book of Pictures*, 10 October 1879.
[3] Brett, *Three Months on the Scottish Coast*, 1886 p.10.
[4] Ibid., p.8.
[5] Ibid., p.8.
[6] Ibid., p.10.
[7] Ibid.
[8] *Early Travels*, 21 September 1879.
[9] Ibid., 5 October l879.
[10] Ibid., 1 October 1882.
[11] Ibid., 10 September 1882.
[12] Letter from John Brett to his brother Arthur (affectionately known as *Bat*), 5 February 1896 (Private Collection).
[13] *Early Travels*, 10 September 1882.

Many of the comments Brett and his wife Mary made, in the manuscript journal they jointly kept to chart their travels with the children each summer, reflect the simple pleasures of parenthood. Of Tenby, Mary Brett for example noted: 'It is an excellent bathing place for children, and all who are not good swimmers being so very safe; the beach is very flat and the water in good weather is smooth and shallow; it is in fact a perfect place for children. The sand at low water is quite delightful, it soon dries and is beautifully firm and generally there are a good many very pretty shells to be found'.[13] Thus Brett's later concentration upon sea painting enabled him to combine his

John Brett – the Pre-Raphaelite Years

In May 1859, in its review of the Academy summer exhibition, the *Athenaeum* welcomed a 'singular work of a rather crotchetty [sic] genius, – Mr Brett's *Val d'Aosta*', a painting that was claimed as 'literally the first large historical landscape painted on P.R.B. principles' (fig. 4).[1] Clearly Brett's particular vision as a painter who was adapting the principles of Pre-Raphaelitism to the art of landscape was being recognised, although this was just three years after the commencement of his career as an exhibiting artist. It was perhaps also the case that his personal reputation as a bluff and occasionally obstreperous individual was established. Years later William Michael Rossetti confirmed the consensus view of Brett as hard to get on with when he referred to him as 'a man of rather downright self-centred tone'.[2]

For a painter whose ostensible purpose was the transcription of the face of nature and the physical world it is remarkable what strength of feeling his works aroused, and how they remain to this day challenging of our preconceptions. Brett was at odds with the world; something of his own unsettled personality, combined with great powers of mental determination, entered his art, which at least in his early years is curiously erratic in its objectives but always fascinating for its obsessive character. He was slow to settle into a professional routine, or really to establish a specialisation, and only in middle age (from about 1870 onwards) did he allow himself to become known for a particular type of work – the marine and coastal subject – and manner. It is a commentary on the commercial nature of the Victorian art world that this eventual willingness to conform to a brand style brought Brett great prosperity for a while, and the prized election as an Associate of the Royal Academy, but that before the end of his life the same form of production had fallen out of fashion.

John Brett's childhood was peripatetic, the result of frequent changes of posting for his father Captain Charles Curtis Brett,[3] who was an army veterinarian. Brett was born on 8 December 1831 (not 1830 as sometimes stated) at Bletchingley in Surrey, a village at the foot of the North Downs. The Bretts lived for a period in Dublin, and then in 1846 Charles Brett was transferred to the Cavalry depot at Maidstone. Brett's later childhood was spent in the Kentish countryside,[4] living with his siblings Rosa,[5] Theodore, Arthur and Edwin, and their mother Ann.[6] As a child he was intense and morbidly religious, and there was an idea that he would be likely to become a clergyman.[7]

Brett first studied drawing while the family were living in Dublin. In 1851 he received instruction from the watercolourist James Duffield Harding.[8] Landscape drawings survive from a tour that Brett made to the English Lakes that year, and these indicate that he was already a competent draughtsman. He received commissions to paint views of country houses, which were perhaps his first professional undertakings, and gave drawing classes to young ladies. At about this time Brett also made contact with Richard Redgrave,[9] who encouraged him to draw from the antique at the British Museum. In April 1852 he was laying plans for his career: 'I at once formed the unopposed resolution of entering the R. Academy as a student DV next December', with the intention of trying 'for admission to one of the W-Colour Societies or bear up for an Associateship in the Academy'.[10]

While a student at the Royal Academy schools Brett came under the influence of Pre-Raphaelitism. On 20 May 1852 he described in his diary what seems to have been his first response to the writings of John Ruskin: 'The day before I got Ruskin's pamphlet on Pre-Raphaelitism and read it through. Gloriously written and containing much earnest, sound, healthy truth, but much also that is false and senseless - wrong'.[11] From the start therefore Brett showed himself as receptive to Ruskin's ideas but no mere cipher or unthinking acolyte of his principles.

Fig. 1, *Portrait of Mrs Coventry Patmore*, c. 1856, Ashmolean Museum, Oxford

Brett's activities from the time of his enrolment at the schools through to his first appearance in public exhibitions – from 1853 to 1856 – are inadequately documented. He was short of money, so much so that he gave up his lodgings with Charles Lucy in Albert Street, Camden Town, because he could not pay the rent. An attempt to put his finances straight by consigning a batch of his paintings to an auction sale in the autumn of 1856 was an abject failure, with the works being bought in or sold for derisive prices. The need to raise money prompted him to design, patent and attempt to market a sketching seat, adapted either for oil or watercolour painting. Sales, however, were few, and this was despite the endorsement of the product by the *Art Journal*.[13] He had various female students, but a propensity to fall in love with them caused mutual discomfiture and disrupted the courses of instruction.

Brett made his professional debut at the Royal Academy in 1856, exhibiting three portraits,[14] while the following year his genre subject *Faces in the Fire* was shown.[15] During the second half of the 1850s he became a familiar figure on the fringe of the Pre-Raphaelite circle, participating in both the Russell Place exhibition of Pre-Raphaelite art in 1857[16] and the American touring exhibition of 1857–8.[17] In 1858 he was a founder member of the Hogarth Club.[18] The fine portrait drawings that Brett made of fellow Pre-Raphaelite artists include one of Arthur Hughes (National Portrait Gallery, London), of 1858, and another of Alexander Munro (Private Collection), of 1861. Over a period of about two years from early in 1857 Brett seems to have been romantically drawn to Christina Rossetti.[19] An unfinished portrait of her by Brett[20] survives in the collection of a descendant of the artist.

Direct contact with the inner Pre-Raphaelite circle seems to have come about as a result of a friendship with the poet Coventry Patmore and his wife Emily (fig. 1), to whose house in Camden Town Brett became a frequent visitor from about October 1852. Sometime during the winter of 1852–3 Brett was introduced by Patmore to William Holman Hunt, and the following May he described the momentum with which he was shifting towards a progressive style of art: 'I am going on fast towards Preraphaelitism – Millais and Hunt are truly fine fellows. I greatly admire and honor them – Have resolved in future to go through severe course of training and close childlike study of nature. In short to follow their steps'.[12]

In addition to the portraits and figurative subjects that Brett painted in the mid-1850s, he also had landscape painting in mind. Possibly his first attempt at a landscape subject had been a view of Derwent Water, which he attempted to put together on the basis of sketches presumably made during his visit to the Lakes in 1851. The difficulties he had with this must have speeded the realisation that he needed to work directly from nature to achieve naturalistic effect. This was one of the repeated themes of the successive volumes of Ruskin's *Modern Painters*, avidly read by Brett and his fellows. Volume IV (subtitled 'Of Mountain Beauty') was issued in April 1856; clearly Brett was struck by what he read there, and in June, 'finding that [he] had about £25 disposable . . . [he] rushed off to Switzerland in obedience to a passion that possessed [him] and wd listen to no hindering remonstrance',[21] as he recalled in a diary entry for December of the year.

In Switzerland Brett met the Yorkshire-born painter John William Inchbold,[22] who was then working on a mountain subject entitled *The Jungfrau, from the Wengern Alps* (location unknown).[23] Brett found Inchbold to be 'a noble fellow, [with] a heart large and gentle [and] an intellect as powerful and vigorous'.[24] He was deeply impressed by Inchbold's meticulous technique and his search for a means of describing the Alpine landscape in as scientifically accurate and informative a way as possible. Thus, he recorded in his diary how, having 'first met him there on the Wengern Alp ... there and then [I] saw that I had never painted in my life, but only fooled and slopped and thenceforward attempted in a reasonable way to paint all I could see.'[25] Brett's *Glacier of Rosenlaui*, (fig. 2) shows a great mass of ice and snow, an eroded mountainside crested by five fir trees (which provide a sole indication of scale in the composition), and in the foreground boulders of granite and gneiss deposited as moraines by the flow of ice. The painting reveals Brett's knowledge of scientific theory about the action of glaciers, notably the pioneering work of the Swiss geologist Louis Agassiz [26] whose *Études sur les Glaciers* was published in 1840. When Brett was back in London in the autumn of 1856 *Glacier of Rosenlaui* excited great interest in the Pre-Raphaelite circle. Rossetti was perhaps the first to see it, and he persuaded Brett to allow him to show it to Ruskin. Shortly afterwards Brett heard from Rossetti: 'Now he writes me that he can't tell me all the expressions of pleasure and praise – and that [Holman] Hunt also was much interested in it'.[27] The painting was sent to the 1857 Royal Academy, where it remained unsold. People generally – at least as represented by audiences at the Academy – were not attuned to this type of exacting landscape realism.

Brett's next work – *The Stonebreaker* (fig. 3) – which he painted in the valley of the River Mole between Leatherhead and Dorking in the late summer of 1857, was a rustic genre subject replete with a complex pattern of moral, social and religious inferences. A boy is seen engaged in the arduous labour of smashing flints into small fragments with a hammer. The open landscape beyond is serenely beautiful, but seems to offer no consolation to the young labourer. A milestone indicates that London is a mere twenty-three miles distant, but again the boy seems unaware of a larger world beyond. A blasted box tree, with a bullfinch

Fig. 2, *Glacier of Rosenlaui*, 1856, © Tate, London, 2001

perched in the uppermost branch of a single healthy stem, is seen on the right side of the composition.[28] *The Stonebreaker* was badly hung at the 1858 Royal Academy, and most of those who commented on it perceived it simply as a meticulously detailed account of a rustic scene. Ruskin, writing of it in *Academy Notes*, felt that 'in some points of precision it goes beyond anything the Pre-Raphaelites have done yet'. He went on: 'I know no such thistle-down, no such chalk hills, and elm-trees, no such natural pieces of far-away clouds, in any of their works.'[29] Various pencil sketches for *The Stonebreaker* bear inscriptions such as 'outside Eden' and 'the wilderness of the world',[30] (a quotation from the opening lines of *Pilgrim's Progress*), thus indicating Brett's

Fig. 3, *The Stonebreaker*, 1857, Board of Trustees of the National Museums and Galleries on Merseyside (Walker Art Gallery, Liverpool)

purpose in representing a figure painting symbolical of man's Fall. Jan Marsh has suggested that Brett may have taken this essentially pious and inwardly reflective subject at a time when he was seeking to win the good favour of Christina Rossetti, who was herself both deeply religious and concerned with issues of social welfare.[31] In fact Brett's own Christian faith remained firm through the 1850s. Marcia Pointon has given a theoretical analysis of *The Stonebreaker*, in which she finds 'a speculative, theoretical dimension',[32] and which she suggests should be seen as a commentary on the briefness of human existence as

contrasted with the immensely long geological history of the earth, of which the spectator is reminded by the chalk flints.

In 1858 Ruskin was fast losing trust in Inchbold as the painter who might best fulfil the principles of landscape art laid out in *Modern Painters*. Instead he seems to have turned to Brett, recognising his extraordinary technical skill, and perhaps hoping that he would be more compliant than Inchbold (or, as Ruskin was brutally to put it, he was 'tougher and stronger . . . and takes more hammering').[33] Therefore, and with the ulterior motivation of causing Brett to return to the representation of landscape for its own sake and as a means of providing scientifically based documentation of mountain, ideally Alpine, terrain, he concluded his review of *The Stonebreaker* by saying that the artist should look for grander and more majestic scenery than the 'Surrey downs and railway-traversed vales', recommending instead 'the chestnut groves of the Val d'Aosta'.[34]

Brett reached the Château St Pierre near Villeneuve,[35] eight miles from Aosta, on 30 June 1858. The painting *Val d'Aosta* (fig. 4) on which he promptly embarked, represents a westward view along the valley of the river Dora Baltea, with Mont Paramont in the distance (although the exact point from which it is taken is hard to establish, perhaps because Brett has combined different views within the overall composition). In August Brett made a short visit to Ruskin who was staying in Turin. Ruskin seems to have wanted to be certain that Brett was not reverting to the type of figurative subject represented by *The Stonebreaker* but instead devoting himself to pure landscape. When inviting Brett to Turin, Ruskin mocked 'that ridiculous Pre-Raphaelite love of painting people with purple cheeks and red noses by way of being in the sun'.[36] Rather taller than *The Stonebreaker*, although almost exactly the same width, *Val d'Aosta* is a *tour de force* of immaculately observed detail, both in the lichenous boulders of the foreground and the panoramic distances. Its human element is reduced to a sleeping girl lying in the shadow of a rock.[37]

Brett was in an optimistic frame of mind in the spring of 1859 when he wrote: 'I have every reason to hope that my Val d'Aosta picture will sell for £450 this summer . . . My picture is better received by the few who have seen it than I could have hoped especially by Ruskin.'[38] Brett was therefore understandably disconcerted when Ruskin responded equivocally to the painting when it was shown at the 1859 Royal Academy. In *Academy Notes* the critic expressed himself pleased that 'any simple-minded, quietly-living person, indisposed towards railway stations or crowded inns' might find out from the picture 'what a Piedmontese valley is like in July', but went on to criticise the work on the grounds that it seemed not to convey an emotional response to nature, and finally describing it as 'Mirror's work, not man's'.[39]

Fig. 4, *Val d'Aosta*, 1858, Collection of Lord Lloyd-Webber/Bridgeman Art Library

Critical responses to *Val d'Aosta* provide a gauge to contemporary attitudes as to whether minute pictorial realism was sufficient to give a complete documentary account of a geographical location, or whether more abstractly evocative devices were also required to convey the character of a particular place. Among others who considered the work to be a mere transcription of nature was John Everett Millais, who described it as 'a wretched work like a photograph',[40] while Alexander

Fig. 5, *The Hedger*, 1860, Private Collection/Bridgeman Art Library

of the meticulous character that he had been encouraging first Inchbold and then Brett to produce – however informative in geographical terms – provided no substitute for the actual experience of the mountains. *Val d'Aosta* was returned from the Academy on 31 July 1859, and Brett despondently noted that it was 'not only not bought but not an offer made for it'.[42] Despite everything, Ruskin acquired it himself – perhaps out of sympathy for an artist whose commercial prospects he felt he had compromised.

Brett remained equivocal about landscape painting in this period, having stated categorically at the end of 1858 that *Val d'Aosta* was to be his last such work.[43] In 1860 he reverted to a theme of rustic labour, taking up a painting begun in 1858, to be called *The Hedger* (fig. 5).[44] This, as he had previously hoped, would be 'more felt than the Aosta'.[45] Also in 1860 he painted a figurative subject in medieval setting entitled *Warwick Castle* (location unknown).[46] This was a critical failure but a commercial success – being bought by Thomas Plint for four hundred guineas – when it was exhibited at the 1861 Royal Academy. The composition of this work is known only from a small sketch, but the conscientiousness with which Brett approached the subject may be appreciated in a careful drawing of armour, now in the British Museum, that he made in preparation for the finished work. Furthermore, he was continuing to paint landscape (and landscape backgrounds to figure subjects) directly from the motif, as may be judged from a diary entry for 30 June 1860: 'Took canvas [of *Warwick Castle*] into park and rigged it against a tree ready for work. Weather promises improvement'.[47]

During the first half of the 1860s Brett made a series of long visits to various European destinations. In 1861 he travelled to the Alps for the third time, moving from point to point around the eastern shore of the Lake of Geneva. A painting entitled *Champéry* (location unknown) and a drawing *Mountains of St Gingolph* (Fitzwilliam Museum, University of Cambridge), each deriving from this stay, appeared at the Royal Academy in 1862. Brett travelled on from Switzerland to Florence, where he stayed during the winter of 1861–2 and where he painted a watercolour of the Ponte Vecchio, which was later purchased by John James Ruskin. The spring and summer of 1862 he spent back in England, where he painted a view of the Mole valley from Norbury Park[48] – a location very close to that of *The Stonebreaker*. He returned to

Gilchrist clearly held Ruskin responsible for the artist's wasted efforts, for in his view the work was 'truly an epitaphical gravestone for Post-Ruskinism; all Mr Brett has now to do is to nurture such elements of the poetic as lie dormant within him by combining the study of our best wood-scape painters, such as Shakespeare and Wordsworth . . . but, above all let him especially eschew the fantastic theories of Mr John Ruskin.'[41] The fact is Ruskin himself had discovered that painting

Florence in 1862–3, a sojourn that led to the extraordinary panoramic view *Florence from Bellosguardo* (fig. 6). In August 1863 he made a sea voyage through the Bay of Biscay and into the Mediterranean to Naples, an experience it has been suggested which first aroused his interest in sea-painting. The winters of 1863–4 and 1864–5 Brett spent in the south of Italy, painting watercolour and oil views of the coast near Capri and Sorrento. While abroad Brett painted what was perhaps his last figurative subject, the proto-aesthetic *Lady with a Dove* (fig. 7) – a portrait of one Madame Loeser, a woman with whom he was romantically involved.

Fig. 6, *Florence from Bellosguardo*, 1863, © Tate, London, 2001

Both *Florence from Bellosguardo* and *Norbury on the Mole* were rejected by the selection committee of the 1863 Royal Academy. Outrage was felt at this manifestation of prejudice against a progressive form of landscape painting on the part of an institution which some at least felt should have sought to support artistic innovation and serve the interests even of painters who were not amongst its members. The matter was commented on in periodicals and newspapers,[49] and discussed within the Pre-Raphaelite circle.[50] Brett was among the artists invited by Holman Hunt to participate in a private exhibition of works rejected by the Academy, which was held at the Cosmopolitan Club in Charles Street in the summer of 1863. Had Brett agreed to this, his paintings would certainly have complemented the overall display, where Pre-Raphaelite landscapes predominated; and among the artists represented were friends of Brett's such as Inchbold, G.P. Boyce, and Henry Moore. In the event, however, he preferred to show the two rejected paintings in his own studio in Pump Court in the Temple.[51] *Florence from Bellosguardo* was much admired there, and promptly sold to the financier and National Gallery trustee Lord Overstone, perhaps partly as a result of the publicity that had attached to its rejection.[52]

Fig. 7, *Lady with a Dove: Madame Loeser*, 1864, © Tate, London, 2001

A sense of remoteness is characteristic of certain of Brett's landscapes of the 1860s. *Massa, Bay of Naples* (fig. 8),[53] for example, exhibited in 1864 and showing the rocky cliffs and wooded hillsides of the Lattari peninsula, with a distant view of Capri, offers a view of the coastal topography but observed at frustratingly long range. No indication is given of where the artist may have been positioned, as the lower register of the composition consists entirely of an expanse of water seen in bird's-eye view. This device of Brett's heightens the sense of vertiginous detachment experienced by the spectator as he inspects a landscape about which so much apparent information is given but to which there seems to be no opportunity for physical access. Comparable is the watercolour *Near Sorrento* (Birmingham Museums & Art Gallery),[54] which again depends on a carefully devised handling technique to convey plethoric detail in the masses of the landscape. In addition to these paintings of sea and coast, Brett evidently commenced painting pure marine subjects while in Italy: the first of these seems to have been the work entitled *A North-west Squall in the Mediterranean* (location unknown), which appeared at the 1864 Royal Academy. In line of succession to the Campanian views of the mid-1860s comes Brett's *Etna from the Heights of Taormina* (Mappin Art Gallery, Sheffield),[55] done in 1870 in Sicily when Brett was there as part of an expedition to observe a solar eclipse, and described on the occasion of its first appearance (at the Royal Academy in 1871) as 'a carefully mapped-out scene' in the 'style once known as pre-Raphaelite', which was by then 'all but extinct'.[56] Brett was thus being seen as a survivor of the Pre-Raphaelite landscape school by continuing

Fig. 8, *Massa, Bay of Naples*, 1864, Indianapolis Museum of Art, James E. Roberts Fund

to use bright local colour and give close attention to detail, even when he had shifted from a type in which foregrounds were identified as the main object of interest through to a formula which depended upon stepping away from the landscape so as to see all its elements as distant patterns.

A third type of landscape – not especially dependent on minute detail, although always carefully made, but characterised by circumscription of vision and intimacy of observation – occurs within Brett's output in the 1860s, and is in some way aberrant in the wider context of his career. *Morants Court in May,* of 1864 (fig. 9), is characterised by fondness for the peculiarities of a particular location unusual in Brett's painting. A Friesian cow and calf, with two lambs – one black, the other white – occupy a foreground meadow, while the middle ground is filled with a house and range of outbuildings. *Morants Court* speaks of a new mood of contentment and feeling of delight in the sights and sensations of the countryside on Brett's part. The prancing calf is the happiest motif in a Brett painting since the *Stonebreaker*'s puppy, and the affection with which Brett painted the incidental detail of the architecture is reminiscent of the watercolours of his friend George Price Boyce.[57] It is worth saying that F. G. Stephens's description of the painting in the *Athenaeum* - 'artless to the degree . . . an exquisite reflexion [sic] of nature, almost a diagram, not a picture'[58] echoes the terms in which Boyce's exhibited drawings were habitually described, so perhaps a connection was perceived by contemporary commentators. The lost *Through the Turnips* (exhibited at the Academy in 1867, and probably a watercolour) may have been another subject of this intimate and affectionate type.

Two watercolours - *River Scene, near Goring-on-Thames* (Whitworth Art Gallery, University of Manchester)[59] of 1865, and *February in the Isle of Wight* (Birmingham Museums & Art Gallery)[60] of 1866 - are poignant meditations on landscapes which might have been dreamed of rather than experienced in reality. Towards the end of the decade (and the end of this phase of intense creativity) Brett stayed in Great Yarmouth in Norfolk, where he produced two further watercolours which express the attraction that he felt at this time for the diurnal aspects of an inhabited topography. One of these – *Entrance to Yarmouth Harbour*[61] – was shown at the Royal Academy in 1869, while the other which was

Fig. 9, *Morants Court in May*, 1864, Private Collection

called *Trawling Smacks at Yarmouth* (fig. 10) appeared at the so-called 'Special Select Supplementary Exhibition of Pictures'[62] of the same year. In this last drawing figures are seen at work, painting the hulls of their fishing boats, and sitting around on the quays, and once again a quiet and unselfconscious pleasure is taken in the observation of the passing scene in the most direct and immediate terms. The word Pre-Raphaelite might still be used to describe drawings of this type, on account of their continuing attention to the careful delineation of the forms of nature as observed and their delicious and intense quality of colour. It would seem, however, that all didactic or symbolical purpose had ebbed away.

Brett was a man of powerful intellect. Ruskin quoted a remark of Brett's in the fifth volume of *Modern Painters* (1860), describing him as 'one of my keenest-minded friends'.[63] However, a while later a breach occurred between Brett and Ruskin when the two men argued about a point of science. In 1865 the latter had had cause to write to Rossetti (who had himself taken to complaining about Brett): 'I will associate with no man who does not more or less accept my own estimate of myself. For instance, Brett told me, a year ago, that a statement of mine respecting a scientific matter (which I knew *à fond* before he was born) was "bosh". I told him in return he was a fool; he left the house, and I will not see him again "until he is wiser".'[64]

Brett was particularly interested in astronomy and from a young age had made astronomical observations. A year after the expedition to Sicily to observe the solar eclipse, he was elected to the Royal Astronomical Society, regularly publishing accounts of his observations thereafter and making careful drawings of lunar craters. Brett seems to have drawn the conclusion that if the origin and construction of the physical world was to be understood in scientific terms, biblical explanations were redundant. Thus, in the course of the 1860s, the Christian faith that he had previously embraced with such piety seems to have been undermined, and eventually he adopted a determined atheism.

Attitudes to Brett's work have come a long way in the last half-century or so. In 1948 John Gere likened the stimulation that Brett received from Ruskin to 'overwinding on a watch: it is as though some spring inside him were broken, for he never again achieved anything at all comparable to *The Stonebreaker* or the *Val d'Aosta*.'[65] This may be true – the two paintings specified, along with the Tate's *Glacier of Rosenlaui*, are masterpieces – but it does seem to imply a cataclysmic eclipse of talent in 1859 which is confounded by the sheer quality and ambition of paintings such as *Florence from Bellosguardo* or *Massa, Bay of Naples*. Ruskin berated Brett for 'painting large studies by way of pictures [which] was simply ridiculous',[66] and in 1875 concluded that since the time of *The Stonebreaker* Brett '[had] gained nothing – rather, I fear, lost, in subtlety of execution, and necessitates the decline of his future power by persistently covering too large canvas. There is no occasion that a geological study should also be a geological map . . .'[67] Allen Staley, in his seminal *The Pre-Raphaelite Landscape*, of 1973, gave a detailed discussion of Brett's career in the 1860s, finding pictorial virtues in works such as *Morants Court* and *River Scene, near Goring-on-Thames*, and lamented the loss of so many other paintings from this period. Thus a more even and open-minded account of the trajectory of Brett's career was offered. However, even then it seemed reasonable to propose the large pure marine painting *From the Dorsetshire Cliffs* (Tate) as representative of 'all of Brett's paintings for the remaining two-thirds of his professional life'.[68]

The requisite physical labour and mental concentration of Pre-Raphaelite landscape painting in the open air made it an artistic endeavour to be undertaken by young men and women, who were

Fig. 10, *Trawlers under repair, Yarmouth*, 1868, British Museum

impassioned by a love of the physical landscape and a willingness to endure discomfort. All of the painters who we regard as members of this group tended eventually to move away from such intensities, but in the process discovered ways of responding in aesthetic terms to nature and the landscape. Brett's later Academy pictures, and their associated preparatory sketches - with their bravura patterns of handling and rich colour and their ecstatic love of places and natural formations that the artist had known and studied so well - can now be considered in their own right, but perhaps be seen also as the eventual outcome of a long and complex artistic evolution.[69]

Christopher Newall

[1] *Athenaeum*, 14 May 1859, p.652.

[2] William Michael Rossetti, *Some Reminiscences*, 2 vols, London, 1906, I, p.90.

[3] 1789-1865. Appointed as a veterinary-surgeon to Twelfth Lancers in 1833, and promoted veterinary-surgeon 'of the first class' in 1859.

[4] During Brett's childhood they lived first at Penenden Heath and later at Boxley, both villages close to Maidstone. In 1858 the Brett parents moved to Detling, where both John and Rosa Brett often stayed at Lynchfield House, along the front of which ran the ancient Pilgrim's Way. This handsome residence (now demolished) was given up in 1860 when money was short after Brett's father was stood down on half pay.

[5] 1829-1882. Rosa Brett was a painter of Pre-Raphaelite landscape and animal subjects. She and John were very close, living together in London for periods. On one occasion John described her in a letter as 'ardent, impulsive and unbendable' (Cordingly, p.5). Rosa's most remarkable painting, *The Hayloft* (Private Collection), was exhibited under the pseudonym 'Rosarius' at the Royal Academy in 1858 (see Elizabeth Prettejohn, *The Art of the Pre-Raphaelites*, London, 2000, pl.55). For biographical information on Rosa see Pamela Gerrish Nunn, 'Rosa Brett, Pre-Raphaelite', *Burlington Magazine*, vol.126, October 1984, pp.630–2, and Jan Marsh and Pamela Gerrish Nunn, *Pre-Raphaelite Women Artists*, exhibition catalogue, Manchester City Art Galleries, 1998, pp.105–7.

[6] née Pilbean. She married Charles Curtis Brett in 1823.

[7] See Cordingly, p.6.

[8] 1797-1863. John Ruskin himself had taken instruction from Harding in the early 1840s, and they remained friends afterwards. Ruskin recommended manuals for the use of artists by Harding, such as his *Elementary Art, or the Use of the Chalk and the Lead Pencil* (1834). Harding would certainly have spoken to Brett about his former student. (Information about Brett's training as an artist is given in Cordingly, pp.7–9).

[9] 1804-1888. For further information, see Susan P. Casteras and Ronald Parkinson, *Richard Redgrave*, Victoria & Albert Museum, London, 1988.

[10] Quoted, Cordingly, p.9. Brett had no idea how long it was to take him to achieve any kind of recognition by the art establishment.

[11] Quoted, ibid., p.11. For Ruskin's text, see Ruskin, *Works*, vol.XII, pp.341-93. The pamphlet was first issued in August 1851.

[12] Quoted, Cordingly, pp.24–5.

[13] In an editorial of August 1853 which concluded 'his apparatus will . . . be a valuable assistant to all who, as artists, study nature.' (*AJ*, 1853, p.207).

[14] One of Emily Patmore (Ashmolean Museum, Oxford (fig. 1); another of the artist's brother Arthur (location unknown).

[15] Although untraced, known from an early photograph. The painting shows one of Brett's brothers gazing into a fire, with his feet resting on the fender.

[16] To which he sent two recent Alpine subjects – *Glacier of Rosenlaui* (Tate, London) and *Moss and Gentians, from the Engels Hörner* (location unknown) as well as another untitled work.

[17] Shown in New York, Philadelphia and Boston, and to which he initially sent *Glacier of Rosenlaui* and a watercolour entitled *A Bank whereon the Wild Thyme grows* (location unknown). The latter was sold, and Brett sent out another drawing, *The Wetterhorn, Wellhorn, and Eiger, Canton of Berne* (Private Collection), as a substitute.

[18] George Price Boyce made a list of the artists – Brett's name among them – who attended a meeting held at Burne-Jones's and Morris's rooms in Red Lion Square to set up the new association (see *The Diaries of George Price Boyce*, edited by Virginia Surtees, Norwich, 1980, p.22).

[19] This episode, and Christina Rossetti's 1860 poem that it inspired, 'No Thank You, John', is described in Marsh, *Christina Rossetti*, pp.202–208.

[20] The identification of Christina Rossetti as the sitter depends initially on a later pencil inscription, but has not been contested. The place name Mickleham and the date 1857 are also inscribed, and it seems therefore that the portrait was made while Brett was painting *The Stonebreaker* in Surrey and when Christina was staying with the Epps family at Warlingham. (See Marsh, *Christina Rossetti*, pp.204–5, for information about Christina Rossetti's stay at Warlingham, which was a short distance from Mickleham.)

[21] Quoted, Cordingly, p.28.

[22] 1830–1888. Although it seems that Brett and Inchbold did not previously know each other, Brett must surely have seen and admired Inchbold's landscapes at the Royal Academy, such as *A Study in March* (Ashmolean Museum, Oxford), of 1855, and *Mid-spring* (Private Collection), of 1856. For further information, see Newall, *Inchbold*.

[23] This crucial painting has remained untraced since the time of its first and only exhibition, in Leeds in 1857. Our knowledge of the work is dependent on a critical account of it in the *Leeds Mercury* (quoted, Newall, *Inchbold*, p.13).

[24] Quoted, Cordingly, p.31.

[25] Ibid.

[26] *Glacier of Rosenlaui* and the watercolour *The Wetterhorn, Wellhorn and Eiger* were seen by Louis Agassiz in Boston in April 1858 and commended for their geological accuracy, as was reported by William Michael Rossetti:

'Professor Agassiz gives unqualified praise to Brett's two pictures of the glacier and the two horns. His authority here is absolute, and praise from him will I hope secure the sale of the pictures.' (Quoted, Roger W. Peattie (ed.), *Selected Letters of William Michael Rossetti*, Pennsylvania, 1990, p.88 n.4.) Brett's interest in geology and the action of glaciers is discussed by Kenneth Bendiner in his article 'John Brett's "The Glacier of Rosenlaui"', *Art Journal*, vol. 44, Fall 1984, pp.241–8.

[27] Quoted, Cordingly, p.32.

[28] Hickox has convincingly argued that this was intended as a symbol of Resurrection, and was an iconographic element inspired by Mantegna's *The Agony in the Garden* (National Gallery, London), which Brett saw in the Manchester Art Treasures Exhibition of 1857, and in which a similar tree appears – dead and leafless except for one single living stem.

[29] Ruskin, *Works*, vol.XIV, p.171.

[30] These drawings, with their inscriptions, are reproduced by David Cordingly in his article '"The Stonebreaker": An Examination of the Landscape in a Painting by John Brett', *Burlington Magazine*, 1982, pp.141–5.

[31] Marsh, *Christina Rossetti*, p.205.

[32] Marcia Pointon, 'Geology and Landscape painting in Nineteenth-Century England', (part of *Images of the Earth - Essays in the History of the Environmental Sciences* (edited by L.J. Jordanova & Roy S. Porter), British Society for the History of Science, 1979, pp.87–108), p.96.

[33] Ruskin, *Works*, vol.XIV, pp.xxiii–xxiv.

[34] Ruskin, *Works*, vol.XIV, p.172. It seems that Ruskin already knew that Brett was intending to return to the Alps in the summer of 1858, and that this comment amounted to an announcement of the plan.

[35] A self portrait drawing executed by the artist on the 1 November of that year and inscribed *Château de St Pierre* is cat. 1 in this exhibition.

[36] Quoted, Michael Hickox and Christiana Payne, 'Sermons in stones: John Brett's The Stonebreaker reconsidered', *Re-framing the Pre-Raphaelites: historical and theoretical essays*, edited by Ellen Harding, Aldershot, 1996, p.110.

[37] Hickox believes that in *Val d'Aosta*, as in *The Stonebreaker*, Brett had Mantegna's *The Agony in the Garden* in mind. He sees the white goat in the left foreground as a type of Christ (perhaps suggested to the artist by Holman Hunt's *The Scapegoat* (Lady Lever Art Gallery, Port Sunlight), of 1854). Also, according to Hickox, the sleeping girl in *Val d'Aosta* takes the place of the figures of the three disciples, while five trees with trunks of white bark stand for the five cherubs who in Mantegna's painting present Christ with the instruments of His Passion.

[38] Quoted, Cordingly, p.57.

[39] Ruskin, *Works*, vol.XIV, pp.235–7.

[40] Quoted by Ian Warrell in Robert Hewison, Ian Warrell, Stephen Wildman, *Ruskin, Turner and the Pre-Raphaelites*, Tate Gallery, London, 2000, p.223.

[41] *The Critic*, vol.18, January-June 1859, p.544.

[42] Quoted, Cordingly, p.65.

[43] See Cordingly, p.57. The statement comes from a diary entry for 25 December 1858.

[44] This work seems to have been begun, or at least conceived, in the early part of 1858, before Brett's departure for the Alps, but then laid aside. I am grateful to Michael Hickox for drawing attention to dates on drawings related to *The Hedger*.

[45] Quoted, Cordingly, p.66. The diary entry from which this quotation comes is dated 31 July 1859.

[46] Untraced since the second Christie's sale of the Plint collection, on 17 June 1865, when it sold for a pathetic £20. D.G. Rossetti, who had by that time turned against Brett, commented on the low sums that had been paid for recently painted works, including 'Brett's pretentious *Warwick Castle*'. (Quoted, Oswald Doughty and J. R. Wahl (eds), *Letters of Dante Gabriel Rossetti*, 4 vols, Oxford, 1965–7, II, p.557.)

[47] Quoted, Cordingly, p.74.

[48] This painting, entitled *Norbury on the Mole* or *View near Dorking*, has been untraced since it was sold at auction in 1864 (and bought in the name of Martineau) until this year. It was offered for sale by Sotheby's in London on 14 June 2001, Lot 37.

[49] For example, in *Athenaeum*, 9 May 1863, pp.61–20, and *Saturday Review*, 9 May 1863, pp.592–3.

[50] Coventry Patmore, for example, wrote to Holman Hunt, expressing the view that, 'whatever may be thought of [the two rejected paintings'] shortcomings as imaginative art', they nonetheless amounted to 'a principle of great interest in the history of painting.' (Cordingly, p.78; Patmore's letter to Hunt, from which this quotation is made, was sold at Sotheby's, 14-15 December 1970, lot 905.) Both Patmore and Hunt knew that the Royal Academy was prepared to use such methods of exclusion to protect the interests of the academicians and to attempt to suppress challenging or innovatory styles of painting. Patmore concluded by plaintively remarking: 'there is some foul play going on . . .'.

[51] For a detailed account of the 1863 Cosmopolitan Club exhibition, see Philip McEvansoneya, 'The Cosmopolitan Club Exhibition of 1863: the

British *salon des refusés*', in Eileen Harding (ed.), *Re-framing the Pre-Raphaelites: historical and theoretical essays*, Aldershot, 1996, pp.27–42. McEvansoneya's view of Brett's unwillingness to associate with this group of artists is that he wanted to avoid compromising his position regarding submissions to the Academy in years to come. This may perhaps have been well judged (if unprincipled) strategy on Brett's part, because works by him were accepted in 1864, and in each and every year through until 1901 (although works by him were rejected in 1865 (a painting of Capri) and 1869 (*Evening off the Menai Straits,* location unknown (see note 62) and probably on other occasions as well). By contrast to Brett, Inchbold and William Davis, for examples, continued to be spoken of as artists who were systematically spurned by the Academy selection, or when occasionally admitted were ill served by the hanging committees.

[52] George du Maurier commented in a letter to Thomas Armstrong: 'Brett whose picture was kicked out sold it immediately, which very likely wouldn't have happened had he met with justice.' (Quoted, Staley, *Pre-Raphaelite Landscape*, p.134.)

[53] See *John Ruskin and the Victorian Eye*, edited by Susan Phelps Gordon and Anthony Lacy Gully, exhibition catalogue, Phoenix Art Museum, 1993, fig.19.

[54] See Wilcox and Newall, *Victorian Landscape Watercolors*, no.54.

[55] See Staley, *Pre-Raphaelite Landscape*, pl.73a.

[56] *AJ*, 1871, p.177.

[57] 1826-1897. One would hesitate to say 'influenced by' the drawings of Boyce. Even so, these were the years when Brett and Boyce knew each other and were friends. They had previously been co-members of the Hogarth Club. For biographical information and images, Christopher Newall and Judy Egerton, *George Price Boyce*, Tate Gallery, London, 1987.

[58] *Athenaeum*, 20 May 1865, p.689.

[59] See Wilcox and Newall, *Victorian Landscape Watercolors*, no.60.

[60] See Wilcox and Newall, *Victorian Landscape Watercolors*, no.64.

[61] Probably the drawing called *View at Great Yarmouth*, now in a private collection, which appears in Christopher Newall, *Victorian Watercolours*, Oxford, 1987, pl.48.

[62] At the 'Special Supplementary Exhibition' it joined among other works rejected at the 1869 Academy, Brett's *Evening off the Menai Straits*. This was one of the earliest Welsh or Welsh-coastal subjects that he painted, and was, according to the *Art Journal*, a 'study of calm opalescent ocean' that was 'supremely lovely', and which would 'alone reward a visit to these supplemental galleries.' (*AJ*, 1869, p.223).

[63] Ruskin, *Works*, vol.VII, p.360.

[64] Ruskin, *Works*, vol.XXXVI, pp.493–4.

[65] Robin Ironside and John Gere, *Pre-Raphaelite Painters*, London, 1948, p.46.

[66] Ruskin, *Works*, vol.XXXVI, p.441.

[67] Ruskin, *Works*, vol.XIV, p.293.

[68] Staley, *The Pre-Raphaelite Landscape*, p.136.

[69] I am very grateful to both Michael Hickox and Allen Staley, each of whom has read this essay in draft and has shared with me his most interesting ideas about the artist. I have enjoyed reading and learnt much from the PhD theses of both David Cordingly and David Alan Lewis, each of whom has made an enormous contribution to our knowledge of Brett. My thanks go also to Ann Sumner and Helen Waters for very helpful editorial suggestions.

John Brett in Wales

Every summer John Brett and his family left London and headed for the coast. Sometimes they went to Cornwall, sometimes to Scotland, but most often they went to Wales. They would rent a cottage for two or three months within sight of the sea and while the children played on the beach, Brett went to work. He painted numerous oil sketches of rocky shores and views from the cliffs, and he filled his sketchbooks with carefully annotated drawings. These provided the raw material for the large paintings which he worked on during the winter months in his studio in Harley Street or at his house in Putney.[1]

Brett paid his first visit to Wales in 1866 while he was still a bachelor. He was thirty-five and had already made a name for himself with his paintings of *The Stonebreaker* (illustrated p.18) and the *Val d'Aosta* (illustrated p.19). He stayed in a cottage on the Isle of Anglesey owned by Harry and Georgina Weldon. He had first met Georgina Weldon in Italy during the winter of 1864–65, and had drawn a portrait of her. She was a volatile character who became famous as a singer but her later life developed into a long-running melodrama in which she embraced numerous causes, engaged in endless legal wrangles and became a celebrity after spending time in Holloway prison. [2] Her cottage in Anglesey was one of a group of four called 'Tros-yr-afon' on the south side of the town of Beaumaris. Brett stayed there from 9 to 17 December 1866 but the Weldons could not put him up for longer and he had to move into lodgings in Holyhead, 'Poor man, he will be very solitary there' Georgina wrote in her diary.

This visit to Anglesey was as productive as all his later visits were to be. In addition to filling his sketchbooks with some fine studies of skies, waves and mountains, Brett also produced two paintings, one of which he exhibited at the Royal Academy in 1867 with the title, *Lat. 53⁰ 15' N, Long 50⁰ 10' W*. This was the first of the many seascapes which he was to produce during the next thirty years. The painting is now missing but

it was highly praised by the critics. 'J. Brett exhibits the most remarkable sea that for many a day has washed the walls of the Academy' wrote the *Art Journal*'s reviewer and noted the marvellous truth and beauty with which he had delineated 'the grand swell of the ocean'.[3]

Brett's previous Academy exhibits had been portraits and landscapes, and it remains a mystery why he should have abandoned subjects like *The Stonebreaker* and *The Hedger* (illustrated p.20) which had been much admired, and devoted the rest of his life to coastal views and seascapes. None of his writings explain his abrupt change of tack. It has been suggested that the hammering he received from Ruskin during the production of the *Val d'Aosta* may have been the cause. Another theory is that his meticulous technique was too laborious and time-consuming for landscape subjects of any complexity and that seascapes were an easier option. These may have been contributory causes but another explanation may simply be that in the 1860s he developed a passion for the sea and believed there was a place for the scrupulously observed studies of rocky shores, beaches and panoramic vistas of ocean which became his speciality. His exact contemporary, Henry Moore, had undergone a similar conversion a few years earlier. He too had exhibited a series of landscapes at the Royal Academy but during a visit to Clovelly in 1857 he had turned away from landscapes and concentrated on seascapes. [4]

Brett's first sea voyage of note was made in 1863 when he travelled on the steamship *Scotia* to Naples. He filled a sketchbook with coastal views, shipping studies and deck scenes. Back in England in 1865 he bought a seven ton yacht called the *Baby* while he was in the Isle of Wight and the following summer he sailed her to Devon where he made a number of drawings on the River Dart.[5] In the summer of 1867, following the winter which he had spent with the Weldons on

Fig. 1, *John Brett's yacht, the 210 ton schooner, Viking*, original photograph,
Private Collection

reviewer noted that the picture was hung too near the ceiling to be visible without a telescope: 'probably it was thought that such an instrument was apt to the subject, which is a storm at sea.' [8]

Three years later Brett returned to Wales and this time he came with his wife Mary and their baby son Michael, the first of their seven children. Brett had met Mary Ann Howcroft around 1869: he was thirty-eight years old and she was twenty-seven.[9] An early photograph of her in a family album (fig. 2), and a painting by Brett (cat. 4), show how attractive she was before the strain of child-bearing and housekeeping began to take its toll. Many years later Beatrix Potter was to observe, after a visit to the Brett's home in Putney, 'Mrs Brett, a little,

Anglesey, he sailed from Portsmouth to the Firth of Clyde in the yacht *Victoria*.[6] Again he made numerous sketches of islands and headlands viewed from the sea, and this was to be the forerunner of several voyages he was later to make in the *Viking* (fig. 1), the large schooner which he bought in 1883 at the height of his prosperity.

Brett paid a second visit to Anglesey during the winter of 1867–68 and this time he was joined by his sister Rosa and his brother Edwin. They paid several visits to the Weldons at Beaumaris and spent Christmas Day with them. 'The turkey was too delicious. Pudding overcooked, alas! We were very merry and I sang a little', Georgina Weldon noted in her diary. Unfortunately by 31 December she had tired of the Bretts and was writing, 'Certainly they are a 'orrid vulgar lot; but if Miss B hadn't been born a Brett she might have been nice.' [7]

Brett stayed on for more than two months and the last sketch he made in the area was a view of shipping at Bangor dated 'March 15, 1868'. He returned to his lodgings in London and at the Royal Academy exhibition in May he exhibited another seascape. It was entitled *Christmas Morning 1866; the sky noticed all*, and according to Georgina Weldon was a view taken from the window of the barn at Beaumaris. A

Fig. 2, *Mary Brett*, original photograph, Collection granddaughter of the artist

almost too mis-shaped looking person, worn to the verge of irritation, strikes one as a good woman who has had a hard life.'[10] The remarkable series of family photographs taken by Brett from the mid-seventies onward, shows only too clearly the transformation of Mary Brett from a bright and lively looking young woman to a tired and anxious older woman. Like so many Victorian wives, however, she seems to have borne her worries without complaint, and one cannot help feeling that Brett, who must have been a difficult man to live with, was very lucky in his choice of companion.

It is not known where the Bretts stayed on their visit to south-west Wales in 1871, but by the end of August they were on the coast of Pembrokeshire because there is a drawing of a rocky coastline in one of Brett's sketchbooks which is inscribed *St Brides bay from Solva Creek looking S.E. Aug 31 / 71 1.30 pm*. Other drawings in this sketchbook include views of the castle at Haverfordwest, and the beach at Broadhaven which lies at the southern end of St Brides Bay. The following year he exhibited two pictures at the Royal Academy which

Fig. 3, *John & Mary Brett with Alfred and Michael*, original photograph, Private Collection

were either painted during this visit or were based on the sketches he had made. One was entitled *Whitesand Bay* and showed the wide expanse of the beach to the south of St Davids Head (cat. 7). [11] The other, representing a rock off shore, was *The South Bishop Rock; anticipations of a wild night* (location unknown).

He seems to have spent no more than five or six weeks in Pembrokeshire on this first visit because by 24 October 1871 he was sketching at Barmouth Sands, on the coast of Gwynedd near Snowdonia. During the next three years Brett's summer sketching tours took him to Cornwall, the Scilly Isles and the Channel Islands and it was not till the summer of 1875 that he returned to Wales, this time to the Menai Strait. He and his wife Mary now had three children with them: Michael aged four, Daisy aged two and a half, and Jasper who was only nine months old. There are several drawings of the children in his sketchbooks among his carefully annotated studies of clouds over Caernarfon. The family remained in the area for more than three months. Again it is not known exactly where they stayed but judging from the dates and the viewpoints of Brett's oil sketches and drawings they must have spent much of July and August on the southern corner of the Isle of Anglesey near Brynsiencyn. In October they moved across to the mainland and were based in or near Bangor. [12]

The next two years were taken up with the building of Brett's first house in Putney. His summer sketching tour in 1878 was to Devon but the following year he took his family back to Pembrokeshire. They arrived in mid June and for the next nine weeks they rented a cottage for £2 a week in the village of Penally close to Tenby. Here, on 7 September 1879, Brett and his wife started the family diary *Memoranda of the early travels of our children*, which was intended to provide a record of their annual expeditions to the coast. 'By Mary writing notes one Sunday and my writing them the following Sunday throughout the sketching season a sort of binocular view will be presented, and the vagaries of one may be corrected by the eccentricities of the other.' [13]

The diary reveals the typical activities of a family with young children on a seaside holiday. On fine days they played on the beach, went swimming or took out a boat and went fishing (fig. 4). When the weather was rough they walked along the cliffs at Giltar Point: 'There has been a strong sou-wester blowing all day and a frightful sea

Fig. 4, *The Brett Children in a boat*, original photograph, Collection Patricia Smith, great-granddaughter of the artist

outside Caldy Island.'[14] The evenings were spent drawing and reading. Brett reveals that he was reading George Eliot's *Impressions of Theophrastus* which had been published earlier in the year.

Although he devoted considerable time to his children, this was a working holiday for Brett. He tramped the coast searching for suitable views, he made numerous pencil studies and small oil sketches, and in particular he made preparatory studies for the two large paintings which he subsequently worked on during the winter and showed at the Royal Academy the following spring. One of these was *Sandy shallows of the sea shore*, a seven foot canvas featuring St Catharine's Rock, Tenby (location unknown). The other was *Britannia's Realm* (cat. 18), an extensive view of the ocean in summer viewed from the cliffs near Penally. This single picture did more to boost Brett's reputation than anything he had exhibited since *The Stonebreaker*. A review in the *Athenaeum* described it as a 'resplendent seascape of a calm, with loitering white clouds and shipping, a vast panorama . . .' and noted that the Royal Academicians had agreed to buy the picture with Chantrey Funds. [15]

The painting marked the beginning of a period of three or four years of prosperity for Brett. His annual earnings from picture sales rose dramatically from £577 in 1879 to £2,800 in 1881, and he was able to sell his large paintings for prices between £500 and £1200. [16] His surprise at the change in his fortunes was expressed in the family diary during the next Welsh holiday. On 27th July 1882 he wrote, 'Things professional have been steadily looking up and all anxiety about keeping the wolf from the door has disappeared. All this prosperity is so new and so utterly imagined as likely to occur that I rather go about as if it were all a dream and as if the present life had no connection at all with things real which existed in bygone days.' [17]

Fig. 5, *Courtyard, Newport Castle, 1882*, original photograph, Collection granddaughter of the artist

This was written during an idyllic holiday which the family spent in the small town of Newport, on the Pembrokeshire coast near Fishguard. They took rooms in Newport Castle. Their bedroom had two windows, one of which looked on to the mountains and the other looked westwards over Dinas Head and the sea. 'It is a very pleasant room and the castle wall thickly grown with ivy is the home of multitudes of small birds . . .'.[18] They now had seven children with them, the youngest Gwendoline, having been born in February. All the

Fig. 6, *Daisy Brett age 9½ yrs Newport Castle 23 July 1882*, original photograph, Collection Peter Watson, great-grandson of the artist

children were in good health and, according to the diary, went swimming every other morning. Brett drew and painted as industriously as ever, and on this occasion hired a horse so that he could go on sketching expeditions further afield (fig. 5). He also took numerous photographs of Mary and the children at the Castle and later mounted and carefully annotated them (fig. 6).

In September they drove over to Fishguard to explore, and to look for a suitable place to stay next summer. Brett liked the place for its natural beauty as well as the possibilities it offered for sailing because he was contemplating buying another boat. He also wanted to invest some of his new-found wealth in a property in the area. 'I have made an effort to buy a promontory at Fishguard, that is called in the Admiralty Chart 'Saddle point' which is a superb site for a dwelling jutting out into Fishguard bay between Goodwick and the mouth of the Gwain river.' [19] He encountered problems because the local people were reluctant to deal with strangers but he persevered and four years later he purchased the freehold of Windy Hall Farm and the adjoining land for £2,600. He never did build a summer house there, although that was his intention, but let out the property to a tenant who paid him £56 a year. He sold the farm and land in 1896 for £3,600 when he hit hard times but he retained possession of a narrow stretch of land overlooking Saddle Point. [20]

They returned to London at the end of September and Brett began looking in earnest for a suitable yacht. He and his brother Edwin, who shared his enthusiasm for sailing, examined a number of vessels at Cowes but found these unsuitable and were more impressed by a large schooner lying at the Victoria Docks. This was the *Viking* (fig. 1) which was owned by the Earl of Caledon and had formerly belonged to the Baroness de Rothschild. [21] Brett put in an offer of £1,200 which was

Fig. 7, *Crew of the Viking with the chef in the middle*, original photograph, Collection Patricia Smith, great-granddaughter of the artist

Fig. 8, *On board the schooner Viking. John Brett seated beside the captain standing at the wheel*, original photograph, Private Collection

eventually accepted and the yacht became theirs. Mary Brett later wrote, 'we all thought her a very nicely arranged vessel, and just nice accommodation for us all, leaving a spare cabin for a guest.'[22] The *Viking* was nearly 100 feet in length and required a professional crew of twelve or thirteen to sail her (fig. 7). In the light of Brett's subsequent financial problems the purchase of this magnificent vessel was an extravagance he could ill afford but he no doubt reasoned that it would provide him with a floating studio, and the family could live on her during the summer months instead of renting lodgings.

The first voyage in the *Viking* went well. They embarked at Southampton at the end of June 1883 and set sail westwards on a cruise that was to take them all round Britain. The children became expert at shinning up ropes and helping the crew. Mary was delighted at their healthy, sunburnt appearance and at first found the yacht an extremely pleasant place to live in. During the course of the three-month cruise Brett filled six sketchbooks with drawings of headlands, harbours, and passing ships. He also completed several oil paintings on board, including *Fishguard Bay* (cat. 26) which he based on sketches he had made the previous year. They reached Milford Haven on 26 July and,

as they rounded St David's Head and cruised along the stretch of coast which they knew so well, Brett noted in the *Viking's* logbook: 'The coast from St Annes to Strumble superb. fine variety of cliff and sky here . . . Saw Carn Englyn over Dinas Village but could not see into Fishguard. Made pencil sketches all day. Sighted the Cardigan lightship at 11 pm.'[3]

On the evening of 27 July they anchored at Holyhead, and then sailed north to Skye and around John O'Groats. They called in at Aberdeen in the third week of September and Brett was persuaded by Mr Macdonald, a wealthy local industrialist, to paint a self portrait (cat. 3) to add to his growing collection of portraits of living British artists. Brett began the painting at eleven o'clock on a Friday afternoon and had completed it by Saturday afternoon. [24] The result was a lively and accomplished portrait which Mary Brett thought was excellent.

A few days later they ran into a gale off the mouth of the Humber. The *Viking* was tossed about in heavy seas, which terrified the children and caused Mary Brett to change her mind about the pleasures of sailing. Although they took the yacht to the Channel Islands the next year, Brett could not persuade his wife to join him on board the following year and in July 1885 the *Viking* set sail for Scotland manned by her professional crew with only Brett on board. However the rest of the family travelled to Scotland by train and they all spent a month living on board while the yacht was moored in the sheltered waters of Oban harbour. Although Brett did not sell the *Viking* until 1891 he seems to have stopped using her as a floating studio after this summer.

Brett's next visit to Wales was in the summer of 1887. At the beginning of July he and his wife, with their three youngest children arrived in the Gower Peninsula and for the next four months they were based at Herberts Lodge, Bishopston, a few miles to the west of Swansea. It was another happy family holiday, especially when the boys joined them from school, but Brett was beginning to worry about the falling off in the sales of his pictures: 'There is however a trace of gloom over all at present because of the evident failure of the means of subsistence . . .'[25.]

Brett roamed to and fro along the coastline from the Mumbles to Worms Head and this time he devoted most of his time to painting oil sketches rather than making pencil studies in his sketchbook. When they returned to London on 10 October he recorded in his studio

Fig. 9, *Aberporth looking west*, 1891, Private Collection

logbook that he had completed two finished paintings and thirty- five oil sketches. [26] A month later he held an exhibition in his studio at Harley Street of the summer's work. He entitled it *Four months on the Gower Coast 1887* and sent out printed cards to friends and acquaintances. Hardly anyone came, confirming his fears that the market for his pictures was drying up.

By the time of his last visit to Wales in 1891 he was at a low ebb. He had gone down with a severe attack of 'flu earlier in the year, and was suffering from an illness which was causing his right hand to shake so badly that he sometimes found it difficult to control a paint brush. However, he was more concerned about his financial situation. Two years earlier he had noted in his studio log, 'My earnings are not half enough to keep the family, not to speak of the £400 a year their schooling costs, and we are now actually living on capital which was laboriously saved in bygone years.' [27] The first casualty was the *Viking*. Camper and Nicholson, the builders of the yacht, offered £500 and Brett had no alternative but to accept the offer. Bitterly he wrote, 'She would have been cheap at £2000, but the fashion now runs upon steamers.' [28] By the time the family arrived in Aberporth near Cardigan in July 1891 he confided in the family diary that he had no cash balance to speak of and his best work was not selling at any price.

Brett complained that the cottage which they rented was too cramped to paint in, and he found the surroundings deeply depressing. In spite of this he painted several small pictures, such as *Aberporth looking West* (fig. 9). He also made a sketch from the cliffs at Aberporth which was to

provide him with the raw material for one of the finest of all his seascapes. This was *Pearly Summer* (cat. 36) which was exhibited at the Royal Academy in 1893. Brett noted that it 'has a good place in the big room and is much admired by the artists.' [29] and the *Magazine of Art* wrote an enthusiastic review: 'In 'Pearly Summer' Mr Brett returns to the triumphs of his 'Britannia's Realm', the chiefest merit lying not in the breadth of his highly worked-up sea, but in the extraordinary amount of light with which he has filled the picture.' [30] However, despite such praise, it did not sell.

Although he never returned to Wales after the summer of 1891, Brett continued to paint pictures of Welsh subjects. Most of these were based on the drawings and oil sketches he had made during his summer sketching tours. A few were based on sketches he had made while sailing off the Welsh coast. *The Isles of Skomer and Skokham* (cat. 33), which was exhibited at the Royal Academy in 1892, was taken from a pencil sketch made in 1883 while he was sailing out of Milford Haven on the *Viking*. One of the most powerful of his later paintings, *The South Stack Lighthouse; the wind athwart the tide* (fig. 10), exhibited at the R.A. in 1897, was based on sketches he had made while sailing off Anglesey in the yacht *Victoria* thirty years earlier in 1867.

This reliance on sketchbook drawings for providing the subject matter of his large Academy pictures suggests that his pencil studies must have been highly detailed. But although his sketches are often heavily annotated with notes on colours, reflections, wave formations and the direction of the wind, the drawings themselves are usually no more than short-hand notes to record the main shapes of rocks and headlands.

In an introduction to an exhibition of his work in 1886 Brett confessed that 'He believed in sketching only for its use to fix certain scenes on the mind, and considered a sketch to be useless if the picture could not be afterwards produced by the aid of memory alone.' [31] This is reinforced by Beatrix Potter who met Brett on several occasions. She noted that 'he does not paint his large pictures from nature, but from small sketches and memory. He seems to have an extraordinary memory and to paint very fast, finishing a large picture in a few days.' [32] But she also noted his use of photography as an aid. Meeting him in December 1883, soon after he had returned from his sail around Britain

Fig. 10, *The South Stack Lighthouse; the wind athwart the tide*, 1896, Private Collection

in the *Viking*, she wrote, 'He goes sailing about the West Coast of Scotland in his sailing yacht in the summer, making oil sketches which he uses for the colour in his pictures which he paints in the winter months, chiefly from memory, though also assisted by photographs, for he is a successful photographer. Mr Millais says all the artists use photographs now'. [33]

There is no doubt that Brett, like several other artists of his day, was a keen photographer. In the summer of 1882, while they were staying near Fishguard, Mary Brett wrote, 'Today Daddie has been photographing as he usually does on Sundays'. [34] Most of Brett's photographs appear to have been pictures of his children, but on occasions he took photographs of harbours and beach scenes. A faded

sepia photograph of a rocky beach was found in one of his Cornish sketchbooks, and the image corresponds exactly with a drawing in the same sketchbook inscribed *The Lion Rock from Asparagus Island Oct.4. 70.* The drawing and photo are clearly studies for a painting which he exhibited in 1889 entitled *The Lion, the Lizard, and the Stags.* [35] In one of his studio logbooks he notes that among the contents of the drawers in his Harley Street studio are 'a multitude of photographs' [36] and no doubt some of these were also views of headlands and beach scenes which featured in the large paintings he worked on during the winter.

Although some of Brett's paintings have an almost photographic realism, this has more to do with his early association with the Pre-Raphaelites, and the influence of John Ruskin, than it has to do

Fig. 11, *Clouds over Caernarvon Aug 31. 75*, Sketchbook No. 45 1875 – 76 (cat. 5), National Maritime Museum

with his slavishly copying photographs. His relatively primitive camera was unable to record anything moving such as clouds or waves, and yet it is the acutely observed clouds and seas which are such characteristic features of his later paintings. Like his meticulous rendering of landscape features and rock formations, Brett's skies and seas were the result of years of careful observation. It was this eye for detail, as well as his technical skill, which first attracted John Ruskin's attention and caused him to remark of Brett's painting *Val D'Aosta*, 'And here, accordingly, for the first time in history, we have, by help of art, the power of visiting a place, reasoning about it, and knowing it, just as if we were there, except only that we cannot stir from our place nor look behind us.'[37] It was an observation which might equally well apply to *Britannia's Realm* (cat. 18), and *Pearly Summer* (cat. 36), and many of the other pictures by Brett which were painted in Wales or were inspired by his visits to the Welsh coast.

David Cordingly

[1] This essay is intended to provide the background to John Brett's paintings of Welsh views and to set in context the more detailed information contained in the catalogue entries. Nearly seventy of Brett's sketchbooks have been preserved, and these, together with his oil sketches, his photographs, his early diaries, the family diary *Early Travels of our children*, and his *Studio Log books*, provide an unusually detailed picture of the life and working methods of a Victorian artist. This essay and the catalogue entries can only provide an abbreviated account of one area of a life which, in addition to his paintings, also embraced astronomy, geology, the design of two extraordinary houses, and the upbringing of an unusually talented family.

[2] See Edward Grierson, *Storm Bird: the strange life of Georgina Weldon*, London, 1959; and Brian Thomas, *A Monkey among Crocodiles: the life, loves and lawsuits of Mrs Georgina Weldon*, London, 2000. The quotations are taken from extracts of her unpublished diaries which appear in Grierson's book.

[3] *AJ*, 1867, p.145.

[4] Brett met Henry Moore on several occasions and they seem to have been on good terms. On 6 September 1885 Brett wrote in *Early Travels* during the course of the *Viking*'s third voyage, 'Mr and Mrs Henry Moore found us out the other day, and came on board to lunch.'

[5] According to *Hunt's Universal Yacht List*, 1866, the yacht was rigged as a cutter and was built by the firm of Ratsey in 1865. There are several drawings of the yacht in Brett's sketchbooks.

[6] Brett was not the owner of the *Victoria*. There are two sailing yachts of this name recorded in *Hunt's Universal Yacht List*, 1866: one is a 15 ton cutter owned by H. Melling of Liverpool; the other is a 9 ton cutter, owner not known.

[7] Georgina Weldon diaries (unpublished), 31 December 1867.

[8] *Athenaeum*, 9 May 1868, p.666.

[9] In spite of diligent research by members of the family, very little is known about the circumstances of their meeting. The birth certificate of Mary Ann Howcroft issued by Somerset House, records that she was born on 3 June 1843 at 30 Exeter Street, London. Her father, William Howcroft, was a coachman.

[10] Potter, *Journal*, entry for Saturday 6 April 1895.

[11] Previously considered lost, this is erroneously referred to as a Cornish scene by David Alan Lewis in *Pondered Vision*, p.231.

[12] A drawing in Brett's sketchbook (National Maritime Museum, see cat. 5) for 1875 is inscribed 'Michael 'Castle' Bangor Oct 26. 75' and there are other drawings of the family with similar inscriptions. This may refer to a hotel or lodging called The Castle. Penrhyn Castle, a vast nineteenth-century building is a mile outside Bangor.

[13] The family diary of the Bretts' travels consists of five notebooks which cover the period between 7 September 1879 to 1 June 1897. The full title written in John Brett's hand is *Memoranda of the Early travels of our children written for them by John Brett and Mary Brett on alternative Sundays commencing in the Autumn of 1879 at Penally.*

[14] Ibid., 7 September 1879.

[15] The *Athenaeum*, 1 May 1880, p.573.

[16] Brett sold *Golden Prospects* for £1,200 in 1881, and *The Grey of the Morning* for the same price in 1882. These were his highest prices. Most of his Academy exhibits around this period sold for between £300 and £500. *Britannia's Realm* (cat. 18) was purchased by the Trustees of the Chantrey Bequest for £600.

[17] *Early Travels*, 27 July 1882.

[18] Ibid., 29 August 1882.

[19] Ibid., 26 September 1882.

[20] Brett provides details of the purchase and subsequent sale of Windy Hall Farm in *Early Travels* under the entries for: 26 September 1882; 12 September 1886; 26 August 1888; 27 May 1896 and 9 June 1896. Maps defining the area of the property are held by the Pembrokeshire Record Office, Haverfordwest (conveyance plans for 1884 & 1896). These also indicate 'The part of the Farm reserved by the said John Brett . . .' when he sold the rest of the property in 1896 (illustrated p.13). He reserved the right for a roadway providing access to the land at Saddle Point. Presumably he maintained this strip of land, intending that he might still visit the area and have access to the sea (Pembrokeshire Record Office reference D/WW/55/8). The original farmhouse still stands today, but the surrounding land has been developed for housing.

[21] Mary Brett describes the purchase of the *Viking* in *Early Travels*, 11 February 1883. The bill of sale and the *Viking's Log books* are in the collections of Brett's descendants. *Hunts Universal Yacht List* has the following information about the *Viking*: she was built by Camper and Nicholson in 1876; her length was 99.3 feet, her beam 22 feet, and her tonnage 199. (She is described as a schooner of 210 tons in *Early Travels*).

[22] *Early Travels*, 11 February 1883.

[23] Entry for 26 July 1883 in *Log book of the Schooner Viking*, kept by John Brett, owner, from Monday 11th June 1883 to 12 October 1883.

[24] See *Early Travels*, 14 October 1883.

[25] *Early Travels*, 10 July 1887.

[26] See entry in Brett's *Studio Log book* for 11 October 1887: 'Returned to town yesterday from South Wales bringing home 2 pictures 30 x 15 one of which The Mussel Rocks of Caswell bay I sold on the 9th inst to Roger Beck Esq . . . I also sold on the same day two sketches 14 x 7 viz. Distant Devon and Three Cliffs Bay to be paid for on delivery. I brought home a total of 29 small sketches and 6 of the 19 x 10 size and one cloud study of ditto.'

[27] Brett's *Studio Log book*, 23 October 1889.

[28] *Early Travels*, 16 July 1891.

[29] Brett's *Studio Log book*, 5 April 1893.

[30] *Magazine of Art*, vol. XVI, 1893, p.547.

[31] Brett, *Three Months on the Scottish Coast*.

[32] Potter, *Journal*, p.58.

[33] Ibid., p.65.

[34] *Early Travels*, 9 July 1882.

[35] Sold at Sotheby's, 17.6.87, Lot 60, (location unknown).

[36] Brett's *Studio Log book*, 15 Feb 1887.

[37] John Ruskin, *Academy Notes*, 1859, vol. XIV, p.209.

A Technical Note on Brett's Paintings

Brett followed the Pre-Raphaelite painters in his determination to paint as exactly as possible what he saw in nature. Each summer he made immensely productive sketching tours. In August 1875 he completed two oil sketches of Anglesey in a single day (cats. 9 & 10) and during a summer on the Gower in 1887 he produced a total of 35 oil sketches, as well as a good number of larger finished landscapes. In 1881 at the end of a three month stay in Newquay, Cornwall he wrote: 'I had some half dozen pictures done and decided on finishing them rather than increasing the number of oil sketches. The latter number about 40 of 14" x 7" (about 30 are saleable) and 6 of 19" x 10" – about half are saleable. The finished pictures are 3 of 4' x 2' each and 3 of 30" x 15".'[1]

Each of his oil sketches was produced in a single sitting of two to three hours, and Brett stated that he used the same materials and methods as in his finished studio paintings. However, he added that, 'their shortcomings are often owing to the extreme haste occasioned by the pressure of unfavourable circumstances such as cold, rain, wind and dust.' Although the actual size of the sketches was one of convenience, being small enough to be portable, he selected the 'double square' format because he believed that 'all paintable phenomena in nature occur within an angle of about 15 degrees above and below the horizon.'[2]

For his early oil sketches executed in 1875 on a visit to the Menai Strait he used canvas-faced millboards prepared by Winsor and Newton, with a smooth white oil ground on the painting surface and a brown oil preparation to stabilise the board on the reverse. On his later visits to Wales, to Pembrokeshire in 1882 and to the Gower Peninsula in 1887, he used stretched canvases and does not seem to have resumed the use of board supports for later sketching expeditions. The standard size for most of his oil sketches is 7 x 14ins, but he also used the slightly larger format of 10 x 19ins.

Brett generally used Winsor and Newton's materials and many of his board and canvas supports are stamped on the reverse by this London firm of artists' colourman (fig. 1). They sold art materials in major cities across Britain, but we know that he bought his supplies in London before he travelled to the remote parts of Wales, Cornwall and Scotland during the summer months. While at Penally in 1879 and after an unproductive outing by boat in rough seas, Brett wrote: 'The unfortunate sketch had to be scraped off, since canvases are growing scarce. The three dozen 14 x 7 size with which I started having been used all but six.'[3] Brett also occasionally used supports prepared by another London colourman Charles Roberson, who was much patronised by the Pre-Raphaelite painters. In 1887 he mentions stretching a Winsor and Newton canvas over an old Roberson canvas to form the support for his Scottish view, *Ardentrive Bay*, (location unknown)[4] and a sketch of 1885 has also been found stamped by this maker.

Fig. 1, Colourman's stamp on reverse of *South Stack Lighthouse; the wind athwart the tide* (Cordingly, fig. 10)

Brett employed various standard sizes such as 15 x 30ins, 24 x 48ins, 42 x 84ins, for his finished studio paintings. He often adopted the double canvas system typical of the Pre-Raphaelite tradition which consists of two primed canvases stretched back to back primed side out in order to give greater permanence to the painting. The additional priming layer slows down the response of the canvas to changes in the environment and so reduces the risk of cracks developing in the paint film as it ages. *Caernarvon from Anglesey* of 1875 (cat. 8), *Britannia's Realm* of 1880 (cat. 18) and the late *South Stack Lighthouse* of 1896 (Cordingly, fig. 10) are examples of this. His *Studio Log book* shows that he also occasionally stretched a new canvas over an old one to form a new double support. *Ardentrive Bay*, 1887 and *The Isles of Skomer and Skokham* of 1891 (cat. 33) were prepared in this way.[5]

The supports purchased by Brett were prepared commercially with a smooth, white, oil priming or ground and the oil sketches are all painted directly onto this layer. However some of the studio works finished for exhibition have also been given a coat of white priming, a technique practised by Ford Madox Brown and Holman Hunt to give additional brightness to the subsequent paint films. *Forest Cove, Cardigan Bay* (cat. 25), *Caernarvon from Anglesey* (cat. 8) and *Britannia's Realm* (cat. 18), which Brett primed in this way, all have a very high tone, while a pink priming beneath *Caernarvon* (cat. 13) lends it a rosy hue. For the painting of *Ardentrive Bay* Brett records in 1887 that he laid an additional ground with Winsor and Newton flake white warmed with yellow ochre and Venetian red and flatted it the next day with a fan sable brush.[6] Brett would commence painting onto such a ground whilst it was still wet. One might expect the artist to have drawn his design onto the ground before painting, especially in the case of studio works produced from sketches, however there is little evidence of underdrawing to be found in his paintings.

In spite of his assertion that he used exactly the same materials and methods to produce his oil sketches as his finished paintings, there is a distinct difference in the handling of the paint in the two categories of work. This is less obvious in the sketches of the 1870s which have a certain transparency to them, but the application of paint in the oil sketches of the 1880s is quite opaque, completely covering the light tone of the ground. By contrast his studio paintings rely heavily on the use of transparent glazes and fine brushwork to capture the

atmosphere and light of the marine environment.

One of the key factors in producing these transparent glazes was the artist's use of an oil-resin vehicle or medium mixed with his ready-made oil paints. This vehicle also speeded up the drying of the paint and gave it a glassy saturated finish. We know from his *Studio Log book* that Brett was using Roberson's Medium, a commercially prepared copal-oil medium, in 1871, which he later blamed for the deterioration of one of his paintings.[7] In 1880 he wrote while at Sennen in Cornwall: 'The sketching this autumn has been tolerably fruitful. I have been using 14 x 7 canvases chiefly with Roberson's Medium dissolved in twice its volume of turpentine and in all cases painting onto wet white.'[8] In 1883 he records using copal resin and poppy oil with some lavender oil, as the medium for *Fishguard Bay* (cat. 26).[9] In the following year he describes the medium used for *Earth's Shadow on the Sky* (cat. 30) as consisting of equal parts of Mander's Van Eyck copal and Winsor's poppy oil.[10]

In 1888 he developed a new medium of two parts Bell's white linseed oil to one part Mander's Van Eyck copal, which he hoped would be tougher than his previous one. However, after a few days, he complained that the copal resin separated out from the oil and sank to the bottom of the container in a dense mass.[11] There follow *Studio Log book* entries referring to attempts to resolve this problem, firstly by adding lavender oil[12] and then by dissolving the copal in chloroform before adding the other ingredients.[13] This produced a more stable medium, though rather cloudy in appearance. In 1889 he improved the handling properties of his copal-oil medium by using equal parts of resin and oil and adding petroleum as a solvent.[14] He records that one of his north Cornish views, *Harlyn Sands* (location unknown), was the first painting executed in this medium and that he used it too for a painting of the Welsh coast in September 1891. He then modified his recipe for *The Isles of Skomer and Skokham* (cat. 33) in which he used a mixture of three parts copal (dissolved in chloroform) to four parts white linseed oil and two parts petroleum.[15] In 1893 he reverted to using equal parts of copal resin and linseed oil, again dissolved with chloroform and petroleum spirit.

Brett used tube oil paints prepared by Winsor and Newton and Newmans and in his *Studio Log book* describes the colours and methods chosen to produce special effects in the seas and skies. In 1884 he writes of *Earth's Shadow on the Sky* (cat. 31): 'Laid gold ochre and Newmans H Flake white over the sky and painted blue rifts into it with Gold (Ochre) and Strontian Yellow and tinted up the clouds with true Rose Madder and the bank of the shadow with Rose Madder and Cobalt.' He continues: 'I have used in it for the first time Newmans Madder Rose dorée instead of any other madder as it is a better colour. The only Cadmium used is in the bright clouds and on them the Rose dorée is glazed while wet.' [16]

In 1887 he lists genuine ultramarine blue as one of the pigments used in *Ardentrive Bay* but in 1889 in his painting *The Lion, the Lizard and the Stags, Cornwall* [17] he has replaced this with cobalt blue.[18] In a later *Log book* entry he describes cobalt blue as giving: 'a more luminous and surer sky tint when mixed with a little Strontian Yellow.'[19] In the painting he referred to as a view of the Welsh coast, the sea was painted a deep blue with, 'French Ultramarine and Terre Verte, brushed onto an opaque series of greys with a fan brush.' The barley field in the foreground was reproduced using, 'a glaze of Verona Brown and Terre Verte, the lights done with Golden Ochre and Newmans white.'[20] This may be a larger version of *Summer on the Cliffs* (cat. 35). The clouds in *Pearly Summer* (cat. 36), which he based on a sketch done from the cliff at Aberporth, were carried out in transparent golden ochre, Newmans C flake white, Laurie's Venetian red and Winsor's cobalt blue. The sea was painted with transparent golden ochre, and cobalt green in the lights and Venetian red and French ultramarine in the darks, with French ultramarine and terre verte in the drawing of the ripples all over. [21]

Brett frequently records exactly how long a painting had taken to complete and whether he had had to make alterations. In the case of *Earth's shadow on the sky* (cat. 31) he was unhappy with the sky: 'It is as bright as I can paint it without violence but is ragged and rather rude and unfinished, but I can't touch it without ruining its only merits.' [22] However he does record the repainting of the clouds in his *The Isles of Skomer and Skokham* (cat. 33).[23] Although *Pearly Summer* (cat. 36) was apparently completed without much alteration and set aside as finished, Brett considered returning to it again, 'but I may perhaps paint some weak greys into the higher clouds another day.'[24]

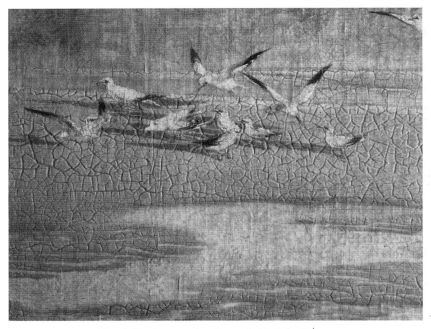

Fig. 2, Drying cracks: *Stronghold of the Seison and the Camp of the Kittywake* (cat. 15)

Varnishing of the finished works would usually take place at least a year after completion, ensuring the paint had thoroughly dried, to avoid cracks developing in the paint. Before applying the varnish Brett would rub the paint surface clean with a raw potato or lemon, or wipe it over with a cloth dipped in warm water. Brett records varnishing *Ardentrive Bay* with Manders finest mastic varnish.[25] Later he describes using his oil-copal medium as a varnish coating for one painting four years after its completion.[26] The medium was also applied as a retouching varnish in any areas of a painting that sank on drying. Of *The Lion, the Lizard and the Stags* sent to the RA in 1889 he wrote: 'As the sky had gone unequally I rubbed over the dead parts today with a little of the liquid it was painted with."[27] These oil-resin varnishes took up to ten days to dry and Brett liked the glass-like finish it gave.

This oil-resin medium has proved very durable wherever the paint has been applied in thin layers. However because of its tendency to dry rapidly, it may be the cause of the strong drying crackle present in some of the thicker applications of foreground paint in works like *Caernarvon* (cat. 13), *The Stronghold of the Seison and the Camp of the Kittywake* (fig. 2) and *Earth's Shadow on the Sky* (cat. 31). Used as a final varnish it may also be responsible for the rather yellow tone of some of Brett's later paintings.

Brett's method and choice of materials was typical of this period of British painting. The fashion for rendering nature in its true colours begun by the Pre-Raphaelite painters led to a deliberate heightening of colour values. This was achieved by introducing a very light-toned ground and by selecting a resin-oil medium which could produce a paint film both deep in colour and capable of transparent effects. The Pre-Raphaelites were also anxious to produce works which would retain their brilliance as they aged. Copal, a very hard resin, and poppy oil, a paler coloured oil than the more commonly used linseed, were selected to achieve the desired durability. In spite of this search for permanence Pre-Raphaelite works frequently develop disfiguring drying cracks and in this respect Brett's finished paintings are no exception. However Brett's use of the oil-resin technique over a wet white ground is still effective in reproducing for us the brilliant atmospheric effects over land and sea that he observed on his travels around the coasts of Britain.

Kate Lowry
Chief Conservation Officer (Fine Art)

[1] *Early Travels*, 28 September 1881.
[2] Brett, *Three months on the Scottish Coast*, 1886, p.10.
[3] *Early Travels*, 21 September 1879.
[4] Ibid., 1887 (no specific date given).
[5] Brett's *Studio Log book*, 1 October 1891.
[6] See ref. 3.
[7] Brett's *Studio Log book*, 12 February 1893.
[8] *Early Travels*, 10 October 1880.
[9] Brett's *Studio Log book*, 1883 (no specific date given).
[10] Ibid., 1884 (no specific date given).
[11] Ibid., 31 August & 26 October 1888.
[12] Ibid., February 1889.
[13] Ibid., 27 February 1889.
[14] Ibid., February 1890.
[15] Ibid., P.S. 15 Oct. 1891.
[16] Ibid., 1884 (no specific date given).
[17] Sold Sotheby's 17. 06. 1987, Lot 60 (location unknown).
[18] Ibid., March 1889.

[19] Ibid., 23 October 1889.
[20] Ibid., 10 September 1891.
[21] Ibid., 14 August 1892.
[22] See ref. 9.
[23] Ibid., 15 October 1891.
[24] See ref. 20.
[25] Ibid., 25 May 1888.
[26] The picture was of *Kyle Akin* (location unknown). Ibid. 4 November 1891.
[27] See ref. 18.

42

Catalogue

Entries by David Cordingly and Ann Sumner with research by Christopher Gridley

All titles contain the original spellings given to Welsh place names by John Brett. The current usage is employed in the body of the catalogue text. Brett's spellings are also maintained in any quotations.

1. Self portrait
1858

Pencil on paper, 20.5 x 13.5 cm (8 x 5 ¼ ins)
Inscribed *Château de St Pierre, Nov 1. 1858*
Peter Watson, great-grandson of the artist
Provenance: by descent in the artist's family through Daisy Brett to the present owner

This fine drawing was made while Brett was staying at the Château St Pierre in the Val d'Aosta. It shows the artist at the age of twenty-seven with the shaggy hair and the luxuriant beard which were such distinctive features of his appearance. Apart from the furrowed brow and the lines around the eyes he looks much the same in the self portrait in oils which he painted twenty-five years later when he called in at Aberdeen during his voyage round Britain in 1883 (cat. 3).

Brett had been prompted to travel to Switzerland in 1858 by John Ruskin who had lavishly praised *The Stonebreaker* which had been exhibited at the Royal Academy in the spring of that year. Ruskin had concluded his review of the picture with the words, 'If he can paint so lovely a distance from the Surrey downs and railway-traversed vales, what would he not make of the chestnut groves of the Val d'Aosta.' Within a matter of weeks Brett travelled to Switzerland and started gathering material for his next Academy exhibit. While working on the *Val d'Aosta* he took rooms in the Château St Pierre, a medieval castle at Villeneuve some eight miles up the valley from the town of Aosta in Italy.

Head of Edwin Brett
Beaumaris
Dec 1 & 2 1867

2.   Portrait of Edwin Brett
1867

Pen and ink on paper, 21 x 16 cm (8¼ x 6¼ ins)
Inscribed *Head of Edwin Brett / Beaumaris / Dec 1 & 2 1867*
Peter Watson, great-grandson of the artist
Provenance: by descent in the artist's family through Daisy Brett to the present owner

Edwin Brett was the youngest of John Brett's three brothers. He had been the model for the boy in *The Stonebreaker* when Brett was working on that painting during the summer of 1857. Edwin was aged around seventeen or eighteen at the time this drawing was made during the winter of 1867. John, Edwin and their sister Rosa were staying on Anglesey and this portrait was drawn at Beaumaris, where the Bretts were visiting Georgina and Harry Weldon, with whom they were to spend Christmas that year.

Edwin was, perhaps, closer to John Brett than his other brothers and in particular shared John's enthusiasm for sailing and the sea. In 1869 Edwin published a slim volume entitled *Notes on Yachts* which has an engraved frontispiece after a drawing by John, and in 1883 he accompanied John on a search for a suitable yacht, a search that was to result in the purchase of the 210 ton schooner *Viking*.

3. Self portrait
1883

Oil on canvas, 34.5 x 29.7 cm (13 ¼ x 11 ¾ ins)   Signed with initials and dated *Aug 22 1883 J.B*
Aberdeen Art Gallery and Museums
Provenance: commissioned from the artist by Alexander Macdonald of Kepplestone, and bequeathed by him to Aberdeen Art Gallery and Museums in 1901

This picture was painted during the course of the circumnavigation of Britain which Brett and his family made in the yacht *Viking* during the summer and autumn of 1883. By mid-September they had rounded the northernmost tip of Scotland at John O'Groats. On the voyage south they sailed into Aberdeen where they met Alexander Macdonald, a wealthy local industrialist and art collector who was in the process of building up an impressive collection of portraits of living British artists. The collection was eventually to include more than fifty portraits of academicians including Millais, Alma-Tadema, Poynter, J.C. Hook and Orchardson. Mary Brett noted in the family diary, 'He asked Daddie to add to the collection, so while we were waiting for a fair wind he painted it, and took it to Mr Macdonald when we went to dine with him on the 22nd. I thought it an excellent portrait, it was painted very quickly being begun about eleven o'clock on Friday morning and finished by Saturday afternoon.'

The result is a vigorous, powerful work and we may assume from Mary Brett's comments that it is a good likeness of the artist. It confirms an observation which Beatrix Potter made of Brett in her journal on 6 April 1895: 'He is a prodigiously hairy person, a forest which invades even his ears and the end of his nose.' Brett had considerable talent as a portrait painter. The first three paintings which he exhibited at the Royal Academy were portraits and some of his early portrait drawings are very fine, notably the self portrait in pencil (cat.1) which he carried out during his stay in the Val d'Aosta, but for some reason he abandoned portraits after 1860 which makes this painting all the more interesting.

4. Portrait of Mary Brett
c. 1870

Oil on canvas, 30.5 x 25.5 cm (12 x 10 ins)
Patricia Smith, great-granddaughter of the artist
Provenance: by descent in the artist's family through Jasper Brett to
the present owner

Although there are no inscriptions to indicate the identity of
the sitter in this portrait, the members of the Brett family
have traditionally identified this as a portrait of the artist's wife
Mary. This identification is confirmed by two drawings by John
Brett in a sketchbook of May 1869 to June 1870, which is
around the time that the couple met. The drawings show a
young woman similar in appearance and hairstyle to the
subject of this painting and both drawings are inscribed *Mary
Brett* by the artist. Mary was the daughter of William Howcroft,
a London coachman, and since she was born on 3 June 1843
she must have been around twenty-seven years old when Brett
sketched her. She appears to be about the same age in this
portrait. Photographs of Mary taken many years later show
only too clearly how the strains of bringing up seven children
and looking after the artist's household took their toll on her
appearance. However her entries in the family journal are
invariably cheerful and full of praise for her attractive children
and their industrious father.

5. Brett Sketchbooks

No. 23 1867; No. 45 1875-76; No. 50 1879; No. 54 1882; No. 68 1890-91

5 leather-bound original artist sketchbooks
National Maritime Museum
Provenance: by descent through the artist's family; acquired by the National Maritime Museum in 1984 from the Jeremy Maas Gallery

Sixty-eight sketchbooks filled with Brett's drawings survive, dating from February 1856 to July 1899. Brett generally started a new sketchbook for each summer tour and filled them with swift, simple, outline pencil drawings. They are not highly detailed studies but an *aide memoire*. They are usually augmented by his written observations including the date and time with notes on observed colours, wave patterns, cloud formations and the direction of the wind. They were clearly an important source of inspiration to Brett when he returned to his London studio and a number of the sketches relate to finished paintings in this exhibition. His *plein air* oil sketches were also very important to his working process and often contained far more detail than the outline pencil sketches. None of his sketchbooks is completely full and most are only annotated on half the pages. They are an extremely useful source for tracking Brett's movements on his summer tours and the locations he visited.

No. 54 1882 (see cat. 26)

Cat. 36, *Pearly Summer* (detail)

No. 23 1867. Sketch made while sailing in the *Victoria* in 1867 on the outer approach of the Firth of Clyde and used later as inspiration for *Pearly Summer* (cat. 36)

No. 50 1879 (see cat. 16)

No. 68 1890 – 91 (see cat. 34)

about Gilton July 22 /79

caldy

Just under cliff there are about 8 waves in the field,

aberporth 21 sep? 91

51

6.   **Menai Straits looking East**
        1867

Watercolour on paper, 25.5 x 35 cm (10 x 13 ¾ ins)
Inscribed *Menai Straits looking E. 5.15 pm Oct 15 67*
Peter, Jack & Gillian Watson, great-grandchildren of the artist
Provenance: by descent in the artist's family through Daisy Brett to the present owners

This is an on-the-spot sketch of billowing clouds over the Menai Strait in the late afternoon of an October day. The inscription, which includes a note of the location and precise details of time and place, is typical of the notes which appear on the hundreds of drawings which fill Brett's sketchbooks. What is unusual is for Brett to carry out such a free and rapidly executed sketch in watercolours because normally he used pencil for such studies and augmented these with small oil sketches. His relatively rare watercolours are usually more detailed and highly finished works intended for exhibition.

Brett paid his first visit to the Menai Strait in December 1866 when he spent a fortnight staying in the cottage of Georgina Weldon and her husband on the Isle of Anglesey near Beaumaris. During the summer of 1867 he sailed from Portsmouth to the west coast of Scotland and back in the yacht *Victoria* and in the late autumn he returned to Anglesey. He made a number of sketches in the area and spent Christmas with the Weldons in their cottage where he was joined by his brother Edwin and his sister Rosa.

Menai Straits looking E
5.15.pm. Oct 15.67

7.   **A Summer Day, South Wales, White Sands Bay**
1872

Oil on canvas, 145 x 84 cm (57 x 33 ins)

Signed and dated *1872*

Private Collection

Provenance: purchased by Rt Hon William Kenrick of Harborne, Birmingham and recorded on 7 December 1874 in the family account book as 'John Brett picture *A Summer Day South Wales White Sands Bay Saint Brides* £150'; now in a Private Collection

This impressive seascape illustrates the famous beach of Whitesand Bay near St David's in Pembrokeshire, with a wide expanse of wet sand in the foreground, a group of cormorants, waves crashing on the shoreline and the string of rocky outcrops known as North Bishop in the distance on the horizon. The composition is dominated by the detailed depiction of the cloudy sky and the reflections in the wet sand below. The painting was exhibited at the Royal Academy in 1872 (No 912) entitled *Whitesand Bay* along with *The South Bishop Rock; Anticipations of a Wild Night*, which featured another rocky outcrop due south of the bay (location unknown). Contemporary accounts record that the pictures were badly hung. F. G. Stephens wrote in the *Athenaeum* on 11 May 1872 of Whitesand Bay, 'It is almost impossible to suppose that those who placed it thus on high can have observed that with such fine drawing and subtle gradation of colour, the proper place for this example was where those rare features of landscape painting could be seen, that is, near the level of our eyes'.

The National Maritime Museum sketchbooks reveal that in 1871 Brett visited the Lands End area, St Ives, Newquay and the Scilly Isles from August to October. He was also in south Wales, sketching around Solva, an attractive village near St David's, St Bride's Bay and later Barmouth Sands in the north. No actual sketch of Whitesand is recorded but Brett must have found the inspiration for this painting at that time. Henry Morley writing in *Fortnightly Review* praised Brett 'for admirably illustrating the artist's resolve to go to nature and learn from herself how to express her moods' and rather than being concerned with topographical accuracy here, Brett is more concerned with atmospheric effect. This painting was previously thought by scholars to be lost and some even argued that it represented the Cornish bay of the same name near Lands End (Lewis, *Pondered Vision*, p.231). However it is clearly a fine representation of the famous Pembrokeshire beach and was identified as such when it was purchased two years later directly from the artist as *A Summer Day, South Wales, White Sands Bay*, by the Birmigham manufacturer William Kenrick, who also owned two smaller Bretts and a Henry Moore seascape. Kenrick was a friend and patron of Burne-Jones and was of Welsh descent.

8.   **Caernarvon from Anglesey**
1875

Oil on canvas, 25.5 x 48.3 cm (10 x 19 ins)
Inscribed and dated *am Wen July 2(?)7 75*
National Museums & Galleries of Wales
Provenance: by descent in the artist's family to Nancy Brett (artist's daughter-in-law);
acquired by National Museums & Galleries of Wales, 1957

Brett here depicts a July morning on the Isle of Anglesey. The view is taken from the fields between the villages of Brynsiencyn and Dwyran looking towards Caernarfon. The Menai Strait is hidden by the foreground hills but Caernarfon castle and the town are just visible in the middle distance. Rising up behind the castle is Mynydd Mawr, the Elephant Mountain, and in the left background are the slopes of Moel Eilio.

Brett had visited Anglesey in 1866 and 1867 while he was a bachelor but in 1875 he spent three months in north Wales with his wife and young family and made a number of pencil studies and oil paintings of Caernarfon and the countryside surrounding the Menai Strait.

9. **Snowdon**
1875

Oil sketch on board, 18 x 35.5 cm (7 x 14 ins)
Inscribed *Snowdon Aug 21 75*
Private Collection
Provenance: by descent in the artist's family through Jasper Brett to the present owner

In this small oil sketch, painted on the same day as the view of the Menai Straits from Anglesey, looking eastwards (cat. 10), Brett depicts Snowdon to the right and Glyder Fach to the left with a coastline of grassy green fields and trees. In the foreground smacks sail on the strait. While *Menai Straits, Anglesea* (cat. 10) was owned by Daisy Brett, this work belonged to Jasper Brett and has remained in the Brett family. This is the only known instance of Brett completing two oil sketches in one day, reflecting the speed at which he worked, during his productive summer sketching tours.

10. **Menai Straits Anglesea**
1875

Oil sketch on board, 18 x 35.5 cm (7 x14 ins)
Inscribed and dated *Anglesea/August 21 '75* with initials on reverse
Private Collection
Provenance: by descent in artist's family through Daisy Brett to her daughter Katharine Scott;
and through the sale rooms to the present owner

This view is taken from Anglesey near Bethel looking eastwards towards mainland Wales, with Caernarfon in the distance on the far side of the Menai Strait. It was painted a few weeks after the previous view of Caernarfon (cat. 8) and corresponds to a similar view in one of Brett's sketchbooks. This is a pencil study which is inscribed 'Valley of the Menai / Aug 12. 75 strong w.wind / midday.'

There are several drawings of young children in Brett's sketchbooks for this summer, one of which is titled 'Michael & Dai in Wales / july 21 '75.' Brett had met his wife Mary around 1869 and by the summer of 1875 they had three children: Michael who was then aged four, Daisy aged two and a half, and Jasper who was only nine months old. Daisy later owned this painting and Jasper owned *Snowdon* (cat. 9), which was executed on the same day.

11.   Snowdonia from Anglesea
1875

Oil sketch on board, 18 x 35.5 cm (7 x 14 ins)
Inscribed and dated *Anglesea/August 23 '75* with initials on reverse
Private Collection
Provenance: by descent in artist's family through Daisy Brett, to her daughter Katharine Scott;
and through the sale rooms to the present owner

Although Brett's early work included portraits and landscapes with figures, the seascapes and coastal views which dominated his work after the 1860s are usually empty of people and any other sign of life apart from a few gulls and distant sailing vessels. Unusually in this oil sketch he has included a prominent group of cattle in the foreground. The view is taken from fields to the north east of the village of Dwyran on Anglesey looking east towards mainland Wales and the rugged volcanic rocks of Snowdonia. The Menai Strait is obscured by higher ground.

There is an identical view in Brett's 1875 sketchbook which is a pencil sketch inscribed 'Angelsea gradated warm creamy ground, rosy in middle, sky cobalt & straw'. On the same page is a sketch of a group of cows. Another relevant pencil sketch is inscribed 'Snowdon from above Bryn Siencyn Church Aug 19. 75 5.20 pm.'

12. **Penmaenmawr**
      1875

Oil on board, 18 x 35.5 cm (7 x 14 ins)

Inscribed on the reverse in the artist's hand *by John Brett 1875* with *Penmaenmawr* and *from the Pier Beaumaris Anglesea.*

In a later hand *Beaumaris* is crossed out and *Bangor* added.

Collection of Mr & Mrs David Barrie

Provenance: bought from the artist by Charles Roslyn Wood; and then through the sale rooms to the present owner

This is a view looking north-east across Conwy Bay towards the rocky mass of Penmaenmawr with Great Orme and Great Ormes Head in the far distance. The inscription on the back of the picture notes that the view is taken from Beaumaris Pier on the Isle of Anglesey, but the position of the headlands suggests that it is taken from a point further along the coast towards Puffin Island, or even from a boat out in the bay.

The three months which Brett spent in the vicinity of the Menai Strait during the summer of 1875 were extremely productive. In addition to filling two sketchbooks with annotated drawings he produced a considerable number of 7 x 14 inch oil sketches like this one, as well as several larger oil paintings.

13. **Caernarvon**
     1875

Oil on canvas, 24 x 47 cm (9½ x 18½ ins)
Dated *Oct, 1875*
Birmingham Museums & Art Gallery. Presented by A.S. Bennett.
Provenance: J.H. Chamberlain; Archibald S. Bennett and in 1921 presented by him, in memory of Laura Bennett,
to Birmingham Museums & Art Gallery

This tranquil view of Caernarfon seen from across the Menai Straits was painted towards the end of the three months that Brett and his family spent in north Wales during the summer and autumn of 1875. Among the annotated pencil studies in one of his sketchbooks are some observations which appear to have a direct bearing on this subject: 'Carnarvon Castle from Menai farm 6 pm Sep 10 '75 nearly dead calm / high water / mountain reflections compact and defined but soft and all detail suppressed'. The annotations continue in detail: 'The air is remarkably clear and the shades & shadows are not blue but dim grey in the mountains. The softness of the little clouds that lie against the mountains is unapproachable. They have a downy character most delicately hinting at blue & gold of a pinkish shade' (cat. 5).

The distinctive mass of Mynydd Mawr dominates the landscape to the right of the picture. Brett also painted a large-scale view of Caernarfon from a similar viewpoint but with the tide out and sandbanks visible in the foreground (cat. 15). The small trading and fishing vessels are accurately depicted. Many would have been directly involved in the slate trade and would have been heading for the slate quay (*cei llechi*) under the castle. The Victoria Dock to the east of the castle was opened in 1875, the year of Brett's painting. It was intended to promote general cargo trade to the town and was the brainchild of Llywelyn Turner, a prominent local merchant and nine times mayor of Caernarfon. In this depiction there is a brig at anchor just in front of the dock. The painting was purchased by the Birmingham architect J.H. Chamberlain.

14. **Anglesea Sand Hills**
1876

Oil on canvas, 35.5 x 61 cm (14 x 24 ins)
Signed and dated *1876*, also inscribed on a label attached to the reverse of the frame
the Anglesea Sand Hills looking over the estuary, although this has been torn and the label is clearly incomplete,
as is the original title. Inscribed on the canvas itself *J. Brett, 38, Harley St*
Private Collection
Provenance: through the sale rooms to the present owner

After spending more than three months drawing and painting views from Anglesey and along the Menai Strait, Brett returned to London with his family at the end of October 1875. He had taken a studio at 38 Harley Street the year before, and since this picture is dated 1876 he either began it in north Wales and finished it in his studio or painted it entirely in his studio, working from his detailed pencil studies and oil sketches. This became his regular practice with his larger canvases as well as with his more highly finished smaller oil paintings.

The picture successfully captures the atmosphere of a hot summer day, with sheep scattered among the sand dunes and clouds building up over the distant mountains. The view is from Newborough Warren on the southern tip of Anglesey looking across the entrance of the Menai Strait towards Yr Eifl on the north Lleyn peninsula.

15. **The Stronghold of the Seison and the Camp of the Kittywake**
1879

Oil on canvas, 106 x 214 cm (41¾ x 84¼ ins)
Signed and dated *1879*
Private Collection
Provenance: by descent through the artist's family to the present owner

This large-scale view of the ancient town of Caernarfon was finished in February 1879 and exhibited at the Royal Academy in that year. The 'Stronghold' is of course that of the English, the Anglo-Saxons and this point was not lost on the reviewers. It was admired by one in the *Art Journal* thus, 'the Welsh town, surrounded with its strong battlements, carries the mind back to times of war and bloodshed, when Norman Castles and fortifications did not always suffice to defend their owners from the avenging sword of the mountain patriots. But the peaceful yachts lying moored between us and the town, and the cultivated fields beyond it, running up to the foot of the swelling hills, across whose sunny face the warm cumuli roll, while the Kittywakes in the foreground sands pursue industriously their calling, all speak of happier times, and we see in this picture one of Mr Brett's pictorial achievements, because the subject is one which lends itself more readily to his pencil.' Brett described it in his *Book of Pictures* as 'Caernarvon from Anglesea near sunset'. The painting remained, however, unsold and was later offered by Brett for sale at Christie's on 1 March 1884, Lot 153, but it was bought in.

The view differs from *Caernarvon* (cat. 13), not only in scale, but in the formation of the clouds and state of the tide which is out revealing extensive sandbanks in the foreground and the kittiwakes feeding upon them. Both paintings include a number of vessels, some typical small trading or fishing vessels accurately depicted with their reflections in the sea. Many would have been involved in the slate trade loading from the slate quay (*cei llechi*) under the castle. Two vessels can actually be seen moored at the quay in the river Seiont. One is a brig with her yards 'cockbilled' to avoid fouling the rigging of the other vessels in the crowded river. In the foreground with white sails are a smack and a two-masted fore and aft schooner and a ketch with brown sails. Local fishing boats and what may be a Manx fishing vessel also sail on the deep blue sea. This larger painting is much more detailed in the representation of the town itself, with figures visible on the harbour walkway, with the crowded roofs of the fortified town rising behind and small plumes of smoke circling up from the chimneys.

16. Proud Giltar
1879

Oil on canvas, 38 x 76.5 cm (15 x 30 ins)
Signed and dated *1879*
Private Collection
Provenance: sold by the artist to F.C.Bovington & Co of Aldersgate, London; and then
through the sale rooms to the present owner

Brett and his family spent the summer of 1879 on the coast near Tenby. They rented a cottage for £2 a week at Penally and it was there that Brett and his wife wrote the first entries *of Early Travels of our children*, the family diary which they kept jointly for the next eighteen years. Brett made numerous pencil sketches in his sketchbook (cat. 5, No.50) of the beaches near the cottage including several of the rocky headland called Proud Giltar which he noted had 'massive slabs like leaves of book' (see below and cat. 5). The impressive cliffs show steeply dipping limestones of carboniferous age with prominent bedding.

This painting shows the view from the beach at Lydstep looking towards Proud Giltar with Giltar Point beyond and Caldey Island on the horizon. The picture was evidently painted at Penally (rather than later in his London studio) because on 21 September Brett recorded in the family diary, 'I have done one little picture of the Giltar Cliffs on commission for £100 for Bovington 30 x 15 inches . . .'. His studio log confirms that the painting was sold on 1 December for £100 to F.C. Bovington & Co, dealers, of Aldersgate St, London.

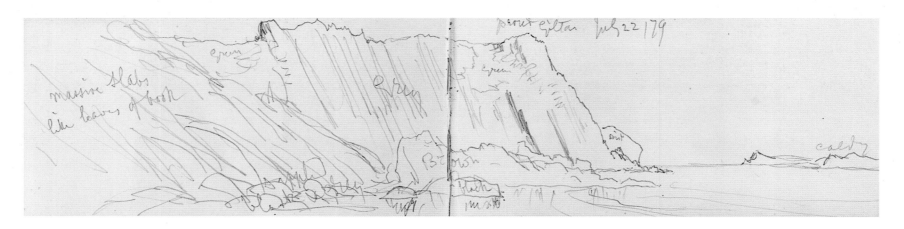

Cat. 5, Artist's sketchbook No. 50 1879

17. Caldy
1879

Oil on canvas, 25 x 48 cm (10 x 19 ins)
Inscribed and dated *Cald Sep 22 79*
Private Collection
Provenance: through the sale rooms to the present owner

Caldey Island, home to a community of Cistercian monks, lies off the south-west coast of Wales near Tenby. Brett's panoramic view of the distant island appears to be taken from Proud Giltar, Giltar Point or some point on the high cliffs between these two headlands. There are several pencil studies of Caldey Island in the artist's 1879 sketchbook (cat. 5, No.50) including one which is inscribed 'Caldy Island from W.Gilton Point / July 17.79 – Hot haze – calm'. A Tenby lugger (a local fishing boat) is depicted in the centre, and in the foreground, a coastal trading smack. This would most likely have been loaded with limestone from the island heading for one of the many limekilns on the North Pembrokeshire coast to be processed as fertiliser for the acid soils of upland Wales.

Brett and his family stayed at Penally for three months in 1879. By autumn the weather had changed and the sea around Caldey Island was no longer calm. On 7 September Brett recorded in the family diary, 'There has been a strong sou-wester blowing all day and a frightful sea outside Caldy Island.' He and his wife went for a walk 'to the top of Giltar Cliff to see the rough sea outside the Island and a fine spectacle it was and we had to hold on to our hats.' As the autumn drew on, their cottage became damp, the children caught colds and the family were glad to return to London, where Brett began work on his greatest Welsh seascape (cat. 18).

18.   Britannia's Realm
1880

Oil on canvas, 105 x 212 cm (41¼ x 83 ins)
Signed and dated *1880*
Tate. Presented by the Trustees of the Chantrey Bequest, 1880
Provenance: purchased from the artist in 1880 by the Trustees of the Chantrey Bequest

Britannia's Realm was exhibited at the Royal Academy in 1880 priced at £600. Unlike the polite but reserved reception which usually greeted Brett's seascapes, the picture was warmly received by artists and critics alike. The President and Council of the Royal Academy agreed to purchase the painting with Chantrey Funds for the nation. Its purchase must have played a major part in Brett's election as an RA Associate the following year. The *Athenaeum* noted that 'Mr Brett's sea picture, Britannia's Realm, is brilliant and admirably modelled'. The *Art Journal* sent a correspondent to interview Brett in his studio and devoted considerable space to a lyrical description of the painting. The review concluded, 'Dark clouds, partially obscuring the piled-up cumuli, betoken to our uninitiated eye a change of weather, but Mr Brett at once explains that it is merely a local disturbance, common in the afternoon, and will quickly pass away, and he speaks with such authority that we at once defer to his better knowledge.'

Brett had started work on the painting in his Harley Street studio following his three months stay in Penally during the summer and autumn of 1879. He drew on the numerous oil sketches and pencil studies which he had made from the cliffs near Tenby. Like *The British Channel seen from the Dorsetshire Cliffs* which he had exhibited in 1871, he aimed to show the vast expanse of the sea. Unlike the earlier picture which was a brave attempt but is rather bleak and lacking in atmosphere, *Britannia's Realm* is a remarkable *tour de force*. The wide format and the aerial viewpoint create a cinemascope vista which, together with the finely drawn waves and cloud formations, and the subtle observation of light and distance, make it one of the most realistic pictures of the sea ever painted. The smacks, brig and two-masted topsail schooner effortlessly glide upon the calm, open sea.

The only comparable works are the seascapes painted by the marine artist Henry Moore, who was Brett's exact contemporary. On 16 May 1857 Moore had written in his diary, 'There is one thing respecting the sea I never saw truly given in a painting – viz, its size and extent as seen from high cliffs – it is truly wonderful.' Both he and Brett succeeded in making good this deficiency.

The only reference to the picture made by Brett in his writings is a brief entry in his *Book of Pictures*. He notes the date of production of the painting as February 1880, the date of sale to the Royal Academy as April 1880, and of its subject he simply records, 'an open sea in summer with a few craft, seen off a cliff'.

19. Dinas Bay
1882

Oil on canvas, 18 x 35.5 cm (7 x 14 ins)
Inscribed and dated *Dinas Bay (?)8 June 82*. Also signed and inscribed on label on reverse.
Mr and Mrs Alfred M. Rankin, Jr
Provenance: through the sale rooms to the present owner

After spending the summer of 1881 in Cornwall, Brett decided to return to Wales the following year. The evidence of his sketchbooks suggests that he made a reconnaissance visit in April and probably stayed at the Great Western Hotel in Fishguard while he explored the surrounding coastline. Early in June he returned to Pembrokeshire with his family and by 17 July they were all staying in rooms in Newport Castle. The small resort town of Newport lies on the coast between Fishguard and Cardigan and was to be the family's base until the end of September.

The view in this oil sketch is taken from the south part of the sands in front of the ruined church of Cwm-yr-Eglwys at the base of the Dinas Island peninsular, looking north-east across Newport Bay (compare with cat. 24). The middle headland in the distance shows Foel Fach at its summit. Dinas Bay does not appear on any maps of the area so, unless Brett was drawing on local usage, he must have made up the title of the picture.

20. **Forest Creek**
1882

Oil on canvas, 18 x 35.5 cm (7 x 14 ins)
Inscribed and dated *Forest Creek 15 July 82*. An inscription on the reverse reads
Newport sandbank Pembrokeshire Coast / by John Brett / ARA
Private Collection
Provenance: through the sale rooms to the present owner

This oil sketch, probably made on the spot, is a smaller version of the more detailed painting now in the collections of the National Museum & Galleries of Wales (cat. 25). It is one of several oil sketches Brett made during the summer of 1882 while he was staying with his family in the popular tourist town of Newport, some seven miles to the east of Fishguard. Forest Creek or Forest Cove, now known as Aberfforest, is just over half a mile from the eastern base of Dinas Island, a remote location. The view is taken from the beach looking west towards Dinas Head on a summer day of sun and clouds. The weather broke a few days later, because on 27 July Brett was complaining in the family diary that continual rain had made it difficult to get much done.

21. **Old Fort**
1882

Oil on canvas, 18 x 35.5 cm (7 x 14 ins)
Inscribed *Old Fort 24 July 82*
Private Collection
Provenance: by descent through the artist's family to present owner

On 27 July, writing in the family diary at Newport Castle, Brett complained that the 'summer is half over and it rains heavily and the wind blows violently . . . I am not able to go out to work'. Yet a few days earlier he was able to make this fine oil sketch of the Old Fort near Lower Town, Fishguard with Dinas Head in the background, bathed in sunshine with deep blue sea and clear skies. The disused fort, built in 1781 to defend the community against privateers, is situated at Castle Point, a cliff edge, half a mile north of Lower Town. The weather that year was, according to Brett, poor throughout August but brightened at the beginning of September, as the autumn approached. Brett recalls that he made four sketches in the first week of September and on 10 September that the entire family spent a whole day at Fishguard so that their eldest son Michael could explore the 'old ruined fort there in which he was greatly interested'. The fort had last seen action when volunteers were rallied there by Lt Colonel Thomas Knox, to man the guns during the French invasion of Pembrokeshire in 1797.

22.   Newport
1882

Oil on canvas, 18 x 35.5 cm (7 x 14 ins)
Inscribed and dated *Newport 10 Aug 82*
Private Collection
Provenance: through the sale rooms to the present owner

This is a view over the Bennett Dunes and Newport Sands looking west towards Dinas Island. It is taken from the north side of the mouth of the Afon Nyfer, a mile north of Newport Castle where Brett and his family stayed from July to the end of September 1882. It was a happy and productive period for Brett. He delighted in the activities of his young children and was pleasantly surprised that his paintings were selling so well. He noted in the family diary on 27 July, 'This is the Hey-day when ones work is a subject of talk throughout the country and when people are glad to get to know us.'

As a bathing place Newport was not ideal. On 28 September Brett noted that from Newport Castle 'We have to walk a mile to the sea shore and never less than another half mile to a place to go in.' However, he notes with pride that Jasper had learnt to swim at the age of seven 'and that without help of any kind'.

23. **Carn Englyn**
1882

Oil on canvas, 18 x 35.5 cm (7 x 14 ins)

Inscribed and dated *Carn Englyn 12 Aug 82*. The painting bears a label on the reverse *Cardigan Bay from the top of Carn Englyn*

Private Collection

Provenance: Collection W.F. Ecroyd M.P.; C.F. Rogers; and then through the sale rooms to the present owner

On the hills above the village of Newport where Brett and his family stayed in the summer of 1882 is an Iron Age hill fort. Its correct name is not Carn Englyn but Carn Ingli (Cairn of the Angels) and it is from this spot that Brett made this oil sketch. The view is looking in a northwesterly direction across Newport Bay towards Dinas Head and Cardigan Bay beyond. The individual rocks in the foreground, which are known as tonalite, are still clearly identifiable today, the only changes being in the covering of vegetation.

24. Cwm-yr-Eglas
1882

Oil on canvas, 38 x 76 cm (15 x 30 ins)
Signed and dated *1882*
Private Collection
Provenance: commissioned from the artist in 1882 by W.H. Smith, Ryland Rd, Edgbaston, Birmingham;
and then through the sale rooms to the present owner

Cwm-yr-Eglwys (Valley of the Church) lies at the eastern, sheltered base of the Dinas Island peninsular. The focal point of the settlement is the ruined church of St Brynach which is one of north Pembrokeshire's favourite beauty spots. The view in Brett's painting is taken from the northern part of the sands in front of the ruins looking eastwards across Newport Bay (compare with cat. 19). The summit of Foel Fach is in the distance on the right. This work was commissioned by a W.H. Smith in the summer of 1882 and sold to him that December for £150. It was exhibited in Birmingham the following year.

25.   Forest Cove, Cardigan Bay
1883

Oil on canvas, 38.5 x 76.5 cm (15 x 30 ins)

Signed and dated *1883*

National Museums & Galleries of Wales

Provenance: bought from the artist by Dr J. Watt Black of 15 Clarges St, Piccadilly, London, in 1882; then through the sale rooms to the Owen Edgar Gallery; purchased by National Museums & Galleries of Wales, April 1985

Brett evidently painted this work in his London studio in Harley Street, and he based it on sketches he had made the previous summer, in particular the small oil sketch entitled *Forest Creek* (cat. 20). Forest Cove, now known as Aberfforest, lies to the east of Dinas Head, the rocky peninsula which forms the eastern end of Fishguard Bay. The view depicted in this picture is taken from the beach at Forest Cove looking westwards towards Dinas Head on a summer day. In this, as in so many of Brett's beach scenes, he pays particular attention to the structure of the rock formations, revealing an interest in geology that went back to his early studies in the Swiss mountains.

Brett's *Studio Log book* indicates that this is the first of six pictures commissioned by Dr Watt Black, a Scottish surgeon and keen patron of the artist between 1882 and 1885, three of them being Welsh views. Brett sold this painting to Watt Black for £150 and delivered it to him in May 1883.

26. Fishguard Bay
1883

Oil on canvas, 61 x 122.5 cm (24 x 48 ins)
Signed and dated *1883*
Mr and Mrs Alfred M. Rankin, Jr
Provenance: commissioned from the artist by Dr J. Watt Black of 15 Clarges St, Piccadilly, London in 1883;
then through the sale rooms to the present owner

Towards the end of 1882 Brett bought the *Viking*, a large schooner which required a professional crew of thirteen to sail her. In June 1883 the Brett family embarked on the vessel at Southampton and commenced a leisurely sail around Britain. According to Brett's *Book of Pictures* this picture was painted in the cabin of the *Viking*, though judging from the size of the canvas, and the meticulous finish, most of the work must have been carried out when the vessel was moored in a sheltered anchorage. The subject matter is based, not on the numerous sketches he made on the *Viking*, but on sketches which Brett made the previous April when he was staying in Fishguard. There is a very similar view in his 1882 sketchbook inscribed 'Dinas Head, April 10 '82 5.30 pm about $\frac{1}{2}$ tide' (see below and cat. 5).

The picture, like the previous painting of *Forest Cove* (cat. 25), was commissioned by Dr Watt Black who paid £300 for this considerably larger work. The view is from the cliffs north of Fishguard looking due east across Fishguard Bay. The most distant headland is Dinas Head and the grey hill rising up beyond is Carn Ingli. The rocks in the foreground are known as the Cow and Calf. The point immediately behind and to the right of these rocks is now the start of the harbour breakwater of Fishguard which lies around this point to the right. The harbour was built between 1894 and 1906 for the Irish sea ferry service to Rosslare.

Cat. 5, Artist's sketchbook No. 54 1882

27.   Caswell Gates
1887

Oil on canvas, 18 x 35.5 cm (7 x 14 ins)
Inscribed and dated *8 Aug 87*
Private Collection
Provenance: probably exchanged by the artist in August 1894 for another oil sketch sold in July 1894
to his dentist Harry Baldwin; then through the sale rooms to the present owner

For three years running Brett and his family spent the summer holidays based on their yacht *Viking*. The summer of 1886 was spent on the west coast of Scotland and then in July 1887 they returned to Wales after an absence of five years. They took up residence at Herberts Lodge in the village of Bishopston a few miles to the west of Swansea. For the next four months Brett was exceedingly industrious: he filled his sketchbook with pencil studies, painted more than thirty oil sketches and completed two finished paintings. As Mary Brett noted in the family diary on 28 August, 'Daddie has done a great many beautiful sketches of the coast, in fact he has done pretty much all there is to be done between here and Worms Head.' This view is taken from the western end of Caswell Bay and shows 'The Slabs' rising out of the beach and Pwll-du Head in the distance. Both seaward dipping and landward dipping bedding planes in the limestones show how they have been affected by folding.

28.   White Rock, Caswell
1887

Oil on canvas, 18 x 35.5 cm (7 x 14 ins)
Signed and inscribed *White Rock, Caswell 12 Aug 87*
Private Collection
Provenance: through the sale rooms to the present owner

This view appears to be taken from Caswell Bay on the Gower Peninsula looking east towards Whiteshell Point. It is one of the many oil sketches which Brett made during four months which he and his family spent in south Wales from July to October 1887. Soon the downturn in the sale of his pictures was to plunge Brett into gloom but at this period he was still able to enjoy the time spent on the Welsh coast with his wife and seven children. On 10 July he noted in the family diary, 'The romance goes on still like a rippling summer sea: year after year the sun shines upon us and breezes blow gently, yet there is no monotony but each week supplies its own pleasant excitements. Surely no ones life was ever so full of pleasure!'

On his return to London in October, Brett decided to hold an exhibition in his Harley Street studio of the past summer's work. He entitled the exhibition 'Four months on the Gower Coast 1887.' He sent out invitations announcing that it would be open on Fridays and Saturdays until Christmas, but it was not a success. Not a single member of the public appeared on the first open day on 5 November, and although a few friends and fellow artists appeared during the following weeks, he hardly sold any pictures.

29. **Bristol Channel**
1887

Oil on canvas, 25.5 x 48.5 cm (10 x 19 ins)
Inscribed *Bristol Channel 6 October 87*
Private Collection
Provenance: by descent from the artist to the present owner

Having spent the summer on the Gower Coast the Brett family returned to London on 10 October. This sketch was made only four days earlier and must therefore be one of Brett's last views painted at the end of that summer in Wales. In his *Studio Log book* he recalls that he returned from Wales with a number of sketches: 'Brought home 29 sketches, 7 x 14 ins and 6 of the 10 x 19 ins '. This 10 x 19 inch study shows vessels in the distance, a large expanse of blue sea and beautifully observed cloud formations. It would appear to be that work exhibited by the artist in early February 1889 at Oldham where he was asking £50 for it, but it remained unsold. In 1897 it was lent via a Mr Bennet of St James's Street, London to St Petersburg, Russia, priced again at £50 less ten per cent for the 'poor and sick children of Russia'. It was returned unsold on 10 May 1898.

30.   **Study for Earth's Shadow on the Sky**
       1888

Pencil on paper, 18 x 35.5 cm (7 x 14 ins)
Inscribed and dated *The earths shadow on the sky 1888*
Private Collection
Provenance: by descent through Daisy Brett; then through the sale rooms to the present owner

This drawing is closely related to the large oil painting which Brett exhibited at the Royal Academy in 1888 showing a procession of craft sailing up the Bristol Channel in a fog (cat. 31). It follows the finished painting in almost every detail and poses a number of questions. Is it a preliminary study which he made in his London studio while he was working out the composition for *The earth's shadow on the sky*? Or did he make the drawing after he had finished the painting either as a record of a picture on which he had devoted an unusual amount of time and effort, or because it was to be illustrated in one of the art magazines?

Brett's *Studio Log book* indicates that on 28 July 1887, while he was staying in Wales, he 'invented subject for an Academy picture 'The Earth's Shadow on the sky'' and a week later he began 'a 14 x 7 study for the same.' Since the drawing is dated 1888 it was evidently not made during his time in Wales but at some point during the following year. It was unusual for Brett to produce such a detailed drawing for an Academy exhibit because he usually based his large oil paintings on the freely drawn, heavily annotated drawings in his sketchbooks and on the small oil sketches which he made on the spot.

31.   The Earth's Shadow on the Sky (the rising of the dusk)
1888

Oil on canvas, 107 x 214 cm (42 x 84 ins)
Signed and dated *1888*
Sunderland Museum & Winter Gardens (Tyne and Wear Museums)
Provenance: acquired by the museum in 1901

Although Brett had first conceived the idea for this picture during the summer of 1887 while staying with his family at Bishopston near Swansea, he did not begin work on the seven foot canvas until 26 December of that year. For the next three months he worked on the picture in the studio of his house in Keswick Road, Putney, where he was constantly distracted by the demands of his seven children and by the plans for Daisyfield, his new house which was being built nearby. He completed the painting on 20 March and sent it in to the Royal Academy in May, priced at £1000, with the full title *The Earth's Shadow on the Sky (the rising of the dusk).* In an entry in his *Studio Log book* on 23 March he recorded his satisfaction with the finished result: 'The work is good and not worried. I think the tone is right, and the colour neither gaudy nor dull. The opalescence of the near shallow sea seems to me nearly as good as it can be, and I have no fault to find with the distance showing a procession of craft up to Bristol in a fog on a belt of calm water.'

Unfortunately the picture was largely ignored when it was exhibited at the Royal Academy in 1888 and failed to find a buyer. As Brett noted bitterly, 'Nobody understood it; nobody asked the price. It went to Birmingham after the RA and was given a central place but there was no enquiry.' The view is shown looking across the Bristol Channel from the Porthcawl area towards the Somerset end of Exmoor. This painting is also titled *Procession of craft up to Bristol in a fog*, a direct quotation from his *Studio Log book*.

**32.   The Rivals from Anglesey
1889**

Oil on canvas, 61.1 x 122.2 cm (23 x 48 ins)
Signed and dated *1889*
Williamson Art Gallery & Museum, Birkenhead, Wirral (long-term loan from Private Collection)
Provenance: sold by the artist to Dr Watt Black; then through the sale rooms to present owner

This view is taken from the sand hills on the southern tip of Anglesey looking across the Menai Straits towards Yr Eifl. The picture is similar to Brett's earlier painting *Anglesea Sand Hills* (cat. 14) but has seagulls in the foreground instead of sheep and is taken from a slightly different viewpoint. Both pictures were based on the sketchbook drawings and oil sketches which he had made during the summer of 1875 when he spent three months in north Wales with his wife and young family. When he painted this picture much later in 1889 he was preoccupied with the building of Daisyfield, his new home in Putney, although he did find time to take his family off to Cornwall for the summer holidays.

The tallest of the peaks is known as Yr Eifl. The ancient pilgrimage route to Bardsey Island at the tip of the Lleyn peninsula left the coast at this point, forking inland to avoid the steep rocky mountains.

33.   **The Isles of Skomer and Skokham**
       1891

Oil on canvas, 107 x 213.4 cm (42 x 84 ins)
Signed and dated *1891*
Aberdeen Art Gallery and Museums
Provenance: donated anonymously to Aberdeen Art Gallery and Museums in 1936

Brett described the inception and subject matter of this dramatic painting in his *Studio Log book*. He started work on the seven foot canvas in the studio of Daisyfield, his house in Putney, in October 1891. The picture was based on a pencil sketch he had made on board his schooner *Viking* in the summer of 1883 as the vessel sailed out of Milford Haven. 'In the same sketchbook' he noted, 'there is a carefully recorded cloud scene which I adapted to it. The motive of the picture is a strong nor-wester with heavy sea and a heavy rain-squall behind an island (Skokham) in Sunlight, and a trading schooner rounding close under the lee of Skomer.' The prominent rock is the Mew Stone: a resistant mass of ingeneous rock called rhyolite. In the background is the Dale Peninsula with the lighthouse seen at St Ann's Head (the entrance to Milford Haven). This headland is underlain by red sandstones of Devonian Age, as is the island of Skokholm to the right.

He completed the picture within the space of two weeks and exhibited it at the Royal Academy in April 1892. He showed it in an old frame and priced it at £800. On 14 August he wrote, 'My big picture at the RA. (Skomer etc) produced a good effect on the artists. Millais, Hook and Watts paid me very memorable compliments on it. But the "Times" after long delay insulted it and no one else dared speak.' In fact a review in the *Athenaeum* of 4 June 1892 praised the 'felicitous breadth and finish' of the painting and drew attention to finely drawn waves and the storm clouds overhead. Brett's original title misspells the name of the island of Skokholm; the work is also known as *The Isles of Skomer and Skokholm (just outside Milford Haven)*.

34. N.W. Gale on shore
1891

Oil on canvas, 26 x 49 cm (10 ¼ x 19 ¼ ins)
Inscribed and dated *N.W.Gale 21 Sep '91*
Private Collection
Provenance: Sold by the artist to Auberon Herbert of Lochaweside Cladich, Argyllshire in 1892;
thence through the sale rooms to the present owner

This atmospheric seascape closely follows the lines of a drawing in one of Brett's sketchbooks which is inscribed *Aberporth 21 Sept 91*. The drawing shows stormy waves sweeping into a bay with a rocky coastline beyond. The artist has written above the drawing, 'N.W.Gale from ... 100 ft alt. Greenish grey sea streaked with multitudes of white festoons in about equal quantities / Just under cliff there are about 8 waves in the field'. (see below and cat. 5) Brett and his family left London on 1 July 1891 and took up residence in the village of Aberporth, a few miles along the coast from Cardigan. Unlike their previous Welsh holidays which had been idyllic, this proved an unhappy time. Brett was extremely depressed by his failure to sell his pictures and hated the house they were staying in: 'The diggings at "Dolwen" (at 5 guineas a week) are so wretched that they only afford me a small dressing room for a studio (about 8 ft square) where it is difficult to paint anything as large as 30 x 15.' He complained that the pictorial material was dismal and although he made some fine drawings of the coastline in his sketchbook, he doubted whether he would be able to concoct anything fit to represent a summer's work.

Cat. 5, Artist's sketchbook No. 68 1890 – 91

35.   Summer on the Cliffs
1891

Oil on canvas, 38 x 76 cm (15 x 30 ins)
Signed and dated *1891*. The artist's name and his Daisyfield address are inscribed on the rear of the stretcher
Gavin Graham Gallery, London
Provenance: Sold by the artist to F. Smallman of Stretford, Manchester in 1894; thence through the sale rooms to the present owner

In an entry in his *Studio Log book* on 19 November 1893 Brett notes that he has recently heard from Manchester that his painting *Summer on the Cliffs* has been sold to Mr F. Smallman of Stretford for £80. Opposite this entry he has scrawled, 'This 'Summer on the cliffs' was a cornfield with flowers in it against a distant shimmering sea painted at Aberporth.'

The picture, also known as *Across the Hayfield to the Sea,* was painted during the course of the summer of 1891 while Brett and his family were staying at Dolwen, a cramped cottage in the village of Aberporth near Cardigan. The fresh, summery feel of the picture belies Brett's gloomy mood at the time and his dislike of the neighbourhood. He wrote in the family diary, 'My disgust with this place is quite past speech . . .', but his gloom no doubt had more to do with his financial circumstances than his surroundings. He had been forced to sell his schooner *Viking* for a considerable loss earlier in the year and admitted 'the blight of the thing lies in the fact that we have no cash balance to speak of, and that my best work wont sell at any price now'.

36.   **Pearly Summer**
         1892

Oil on canvas, 104 x 213 cm (41 x 84 ins)
Signed and dated *1892*
The Forbes Magazine Collection, New York
Provenance: Artist's sale at Christie's, London, 15 February 1909, lot 120, for 105 gns;
Anonymous sale, Christie's, London, 5 March 1971, lot 62; Fine Art Society, London (Agents for The Forbes Magazine Collection)

Similar in subject to Brett's painting *Britannia's Realm* of 1880 (cat. 18), this picture is more subtle in its rendering of sea and sky and has the added interest of clearly discernible human activity in the middle distance. *Pearly Summer* was much admired by Brett's fellow artists when it was exhibited at the Royal Academy in 1893 and later earned an Honourable Mention and favourable reviews when shown at the Paris Salon of 1894. Unhappily it failed to find a buyer in Brett's lifetime.

An entry in Brett's *Studio Log book* for 14 August 1892 explains the subject matter and also indicates that it took him no more than two weeks to complete the painting: 'On 1st August I began another 7 foot picture of an opposite sort of subject. "Pearly Summer" from a sketch off the cliffs at Aberporth dated 27 July 91. It went very well and without alteration during the first week. Then I had to introduce more subject, and so put in the towing incident, "stand by to cast off etc." It was practically finished yesterday and I have a favourable opinion of it. I doubt whether it can be better done.'

Brett took the towing incident from a pencil drawing of a steam paddle tug and two sailing vessels which he had made twenty-four years earlier (see below and cat. 5). The drawing is dated *July 3 / 67* and appears in a sketchbook he kept while he was sailing on board the yacht *Victoria* off Little Cumbrae Island in the outer approaches to the Firth of Clyde. When he submitted *Pearly Summer* to the Royal Academy he provided a catalogue entry which was intended to explain the nautical manouevres taking place in the picture:

> '*Skipper of smack.* 'Stand by to cast off!'
> *Master of tug.* 'Ease her!'
> *Cox of shore boat.* 'Way enough, mates; she'll just fetch us."

Cat.5, Artist's sketchbook No.23 1867 (detail)

37.   Bristol Channel from the Welsh Coast
1895

Oil on canvas, 39 x 76.5 cm (15 ¼ x 30 ins)
Signed and dated *1895*, and inscribed with *Bristol Channel from the Welsh Coast* on the stretcher
Private Collection
Provenance: by descent in the artist's family and then through the sale rooms to the present owner

This picture must be based on drawings and oil sketches which Brett had made during earlier trips to Wales because in 1895 (and the previous two years) he and his family stayed at home in Putney in order to save money. His paintings were not selling and he was finding it hard to support his wife and seven children. Looking back on the difficult years in 1896 he wrote, 'One after another our securities had to be sold to meet immediate necessities, and especially to keep the children at school, so that all our savings have been dissipated and starvation stared us in the face.'

The line of shipping in the distance is reminiscent of his painting *The Earth's Shadow on the Sky,* which showed ships going up the Bristol Channel in a fog (cat. 30). His preliminary studies for this were made while he was staying at Bishopston on the Gower peninsula in 1887, but the density of vessels in that painting, and in this one, suggests a viewpoint further up the Bristol Channel towards Cardiff and is possibly a view from the cliffs around Lavernock Point. This stretch of coastline also inspired the French Impressionist artist Alfred Sisley who stayed at Penarth in 1897 and made nineteen paintings of the area including *The Cliff at Penarth, Evening Low tide* (NMW A 2695).

A Note on the Framing of John Brett's Welsh Seascapes

Of the paintings selected for the present exhibition, just over one third still retain their original frame. One of Brett's earliest Welsh seascapes *A Summer Day, White Sands Bay* of 1872 (cat. 9) has a flat pattern frame with reeded and hatched panels and a large gold gilded mount. By the late 1870s Brett had begun to employ a more distinctive frame of a specific zigzag pattern for many of his seascapes. It comprises a compound profile made in two sections with an outer frame with decorated cushion moulding and a small inner moulding of stylized leaf tips or buds, with a separate wide gilded mount (or flat). The cushion is ornamented with an alternating palmette or tanned leaf pattern of straight edged zigzag. This striking pattern favoured by Brett perfectly complements his paintings and was devised for him by the firm of Dolman and Son, previously known as Criswick and Dolman. They began trading in New Compton Street as Dolman and Son in 1879, the year in which the earliest frame of this pattern is recorded. It appears on the painting of Caldey island dated 1879 (cat. 17). After 1880 they became 'Frame Makers to the National Gallery.' They also catered to a wide range of later 19th century artists such as Herkomer and Alma Tadema.

This standard frame was adapted for each size, scaled up or down accordingly. Even Brett's 7 x 14 ins canvases have these surprisingly ornate frames and large gilt flats, transforming small sketches into fully fledged landscape paintings, as with *Forest Creek* (cat. 20), *White Rock Caswell* (cat. 28) and *Caswell Gates* (cat. 27). One of the finest examples of the larger frame is that on *Britannia's Realm* (cat. 18). A number of the paintings retain an original framer's stamp, among them the already mentioned *Caldy* of 1879 (cat. 17), *Cwm-yr-Eglas* of 1882 (cat. 24), *Caswell Bay* of 1887 (cat. 28) and *Bristol Channel from the Welsh Coast* of 1895 (cat. 37). A label on the reverse of the Bristol Channel states that 'This frame can be repeated at any time by quoting the number 24825'. There are numerous references to the firm of Dolmans in Brett's *Studio Log book*

Fig. 1, *Forest Creek*, 1882, cat. 20 with original Dolman frame

including one in 1894 that states that the frames cost £1 15s each, although the size is not recorded. Interestingly, Brett records in February 1889 that 'Dolman fetched away one of the old Academy frames to clean and size for the forthcoming Academy, as I cannot afford a new frame this year'. In April 1889 Brett writes that 'Dolmans man came and changed glasses and sealed up nine sold sketches, and took away eight of them to deliver to their owners'.

Neither of the two paintings in the National Museum & Gallery collection by Brett has retained its original frame. As part of the focus on Brett, it was decided to commission an exact replica frame suitably aged for the museum's painting *Forest Cove* (cat. 25). The small study *Forest Creek* (cat. 20) which Brett used as inspiration the following year when he painted *Forest Cove* (cat. 25) is on loan to the exhibition and retains an original frame. This frame was thus used as a reference point by the framers to produce a reproduction frame, scaled up appropriately, that could stand comparison with many originals. Two particularly fine examples of the Dolman frame are illustrated opposite surrounding *Cwm-yr-Eglas* (cat. 24) and *Caldy* (cat. 17), as well as an example of a smaller frame around the *Forest Creek* sketch (cat. 20).

Ann Sumner

Fig. 2, *Caldy*, 1879, cat. 17 with original Dolman frame

Fig. 3, *Cwm-yr-Eglas*, 1882, cat. 24 with original Dolman frame

Bibliography

1: Brett's own writings

'Natural Science at the Royal Academy', *Nature*, vol.2, 30 June 1870, pp.157 – 8

'Mount Etna', *Nature*, vol.3, 2 February 1871, p.266

'Expedition of 1870, at Augusta, Sicily', *Monthly Notices of the Royal Astronomical Society*, vol.31, March 1871, pp.163 – 6

'On the Altizimuth Mounting for Telescopes, especially adapted for the use of Observers who have no permanent observatory', *Monthly Notices of the Royal Astronomical Society*, vol.32, June 1872, pp.294 – 6

'On Certain Phenomena surrounding the Sun's Limb as seen in the Telescope', *Monthly Notices of the Royal Astronomical Society*, vol.32, June 1872, pp.297 – 300

'The Italian Report upon the Eclipse of 1870', *Nature*, vol.7, 20 February 1873, pp.308 – 10

'Memorandum of Observations of Jupiter made during the month of April 1874', *Monthly Notices of the Royal Astronomical Society*, vol.34, May 1874, pp.359 – 60

'On Certain Phenomena seen during Eclipses of the Sun, and their bearing on the question of a Lunar Atmosphere', *Monthly Notices of the Royal Astronomical Society*, vol.35, November 1874, pp.14 – 16

'On the Proper Motion of Bright Spots on Jupiter', *Monthly Notices of the Royal Astronomical Society*, vol.36, June 1876, pp.355 – 7

'The Specular Reflexion Hypothesis, and its bearing on the Transit of Venus', *Monthly Notices of the Royal Astronomical Society*, vol.37, January 1877, pp.126 – 7

'The Physical Condition of Mars', *Monthly Notices of the Royal Astronomical Society*, vol.38, December 1877, pp.58 – 61

'Reform of the Royal Academy', letter to *The Times*, 15 May 1879

'The Great Patch on Jupiter', *Observatory*, vol.3, 1880, pp.236 – 38

Letter to *The Times*, 3 June 1884

'On Nude Studies', letter to *The Times*, 22 May 1885

'The Commentaries', *Three Months on the Scottish Coast – A Series of Sketches and Pictures painted during the summer of the present year*, exhibition catalogue, Fine Art Society, London, 1886

Letter to *The Times*, 11 May 1888

'Water-colour at the Academy', letter to *The Times*, 24 May 1888

Letter to *The Times*, 11 September 1888

Letter to *The Times*, 6 November 1890

'The National Gallery of British Art', letter to *The Times*, 23 May 1891

'The Function of Texture in the Arts', *Art Journal*, 1893, pp.117 – 20

'Suggestions for a new Fine-Art Copyright Act', letter to *Magazine of Art*, vol.16, 1893, p.129

'Raphael's Cartoons Criticized', *Magazine of Art*, vol.17, 1893 – 4, pp.295 – 9

'Landscape at the National Gallery', *Fortnightly Review*, vol.LVII, 1895, pp.623 – 39

'Realism in Painting', *Contemporary Review*, vol.75, June 1899, pp.823, 825

'The Relation of Photography to the Pictorial Arts', *Journal of the Camera Club*, April 1899, pp.84 – 6

2: Published writings on Brett

Anonymous, 'John Brett, A.R.A.', *Art Journal*, 1902, p.87

Anonymous, 'Sketching Apparatus', *Art Journal*, 1853, p.207

Boase, T.S.R. , 'English Artists and the Val d'Aosta', *Journal of the Warburg and Courtauld Institutes*, vol.19, 1956, pp.283 – 94

Bendiner, Kenneth, 'John Brett's "The Glacier of Rosenlaui"', *Art Journal*, vol. 44, Fall 1984, pp.241 – 8

Bendiner, Kenneth, *An Introduction to Victorian Painting*, New Haven, 1985 (chapter 3, 'John Brett (1831 – 1902) *The Glacier of Rosenlaui*', pp.47 – 63)

Brett, P[atrick] J., 'Portraits by Pen and Camera – John Brett's Work as seen by Beatrix Potter', *Country Life*, 27 September 1979, pp.948 – 9

Christie, Manson & Wood, Ltd, *Catalogue of the Remaining Works of John Brett, A.R.A., deceased, late of Daisyfield, Putney*, sale catalogue, 1902

Cordingly, David, '"The Stonebreaker": An Examination of the Landscape in a Painting by John Brett', *Burlington Magazine*, 1982, pp.141 – 5

Fenn, W[illiam] W., 'Artists' Houses', *Art Journal*, 1882, pp.57 – 8

Girouard, Mark, 'An Open Plan in the 1880s', *Country Life*, 29 March 1962, pp.720 – 22

Hickox, Michael, 'John Brett and the Rossettis', *Journal of Pre-Raphaelite Studies*, vol.V, no.2, 1985, pp.105 – 110

Hickox, Michael, 'John Brett's The Stonebreaker', *Review of the Pre-Raphaelite Society*, vol.IV, no.I, 1996, pp.13 – 23

Hickox, Michael, 'The Royal Academy's Rejection of Brett's Florence', *Review of the Pre-Raphaelite Society*, vol.III, no.I, 1995, pp.10 – 16

Hickox, Michael, 'The Unpublished Correspondence of Ruskin and Brett', *Ruskin Gazette* (edited by O.E. Madden), 1995, pp.1 – 25

Hickox, Michael, 'John Brett and Ruskin', *Burlington Magazine*, 1996, pp.521 – 6

Hickox, Michael, 'John Brett's Portraits', *Review of the Pre-Raphaelite Society*, vol.IV, no.I, 1996, pp.13 – 19

Hickox, Michael, and Payne, Christiana, 'Sermons in Stones: John Brett's "The Stonebreaker"', in *Re-framing the Pre-Raphaelites*, Aldershot, 1996, pp.99 – 114

McEvansoneya, Philip, 'More Light on the Royal Academy's Rejection of Brett's Florence', *Review of the Pre-Raphaelite Society*, vol.IV, no.I, 1996, pp.19 – 23

MacLean, Frank, *Henry Moore R.A.*, London, 1905 (chapter XI 'John Brett and other contemporary sea-painters')

Pointon, Marcia, 'Geology and Landscape painting in Nineteenth-Century England', (part of *Images of the Earth – Essays in the History of the Environmental Sciences* (edited by L.J. Jordanova & Roy S. Porter), *British Society for the History of Science*, 1979, pp.87 – 108

'Some Water-colours by John Brett', *Burlington Magazine*, 1973, pp.88 – 93

Staley, Allen, *The Pre-Raphaelite Landscape*, Oxford, 1973 (chapter X 'John Brett', pp.124 – 37)

[Stephens, Frederic George], 'Mr John Brett's Sketches', *Athenaeum*, 18 December 1886, pp.832 – 3

Taylor, Simon, 'John Brett's Val D'Aosta', *Antique Collector*, June 1989, pp.114 – 5

Turner, Herbert Hall, 'Obituary of John Brett', *Monthly Notices of the Royal Astronomical Society*, February 1902, vol.LXII, pp.238 – 41

3: Unpublished writings on Brett

Cordingly, David, 'The Life of John Brett – Painter of Pre-Raphaelite Landscapes and Seascapes', PhD thesis, University of Sussex, 1983

Lewis, David Alan, 'Victorian Vistas: An Examination of John Brett's Landscapes, Coastal Views and Sea Pieces 1860 – 1880', MA thesis, Indiana University, 1986

Lewis, David Alan, 'Pondered Vision: The Art and Life of John Brett, A.R.A., 1830 – 1902', PhD thesis, University Graduate School Henry Redford Hope School of Fine Arts, Indiana University, 1995.

4: Primary Sources

The diaries of John Brett, covering the periods 1851 – 56; 1858 – 60; 1860 – 61 'Memoranda of the Early travels of our children written for them by John Brett and Mary Brett on alternate Sundays commencing in the Autumn of 1879 at Penally'

John Brett's studio logbooks:

a) 'Book of Pictures: being a record of the size, subject, price and destination of my principal productions from this year 1879 (inclusive) but not taking any account of sketches, these being recorded in my annual catalogue.'
This covers the period 1879 – 1886.

b) 'Studio log kept by John Brett A.R.A. at 38 Harley Street, London.'
This covers the period 1887 – 1894.

c) 'Studio log, Daisyfield, Putney 1894. Containing Records of Pictorial Transactions, by John Brett A.R.A.'
This covers the period 1894 – 1901.

'Logbook of the Schooner Viking, kept by John Brett from 11 June 1883 – 12 October 1883.'

Miscellaneous letters from John Brett

5: Others

Hunt's Universal Yacht List, London, 1866

Barrie, David (ed.), *Modern Painters by Ruskin,* London, 1987

Brett, Edwin, *Notes on Yachts*, London, 1869

Cooke, E.T. and Wedderburn, A., *The Works of John Ruskin*, 39 vols, London, 1903 – 12

Cordingly, David, *Marine Painting in England: 1700 – 1900*, London, 1973

Doughty, Oswald and Wahl, J.R. (eds), *Letters of Dante Gabriel Rossetti*, 4 vols, Oxford, 1965 – 7

Grierson, Edward, *Storm Bird: The Strange Life of Georgina Weldon*, London, 1959

Harding, Eileen (ed.), *Re-framing the Pre-Raphaelites: historical and theoretical essays*, Aldershot, 1996

Linder, Leslie (ed.), *The Journal of Beatrix Potter from 1881 – 1897* London, 1966

Marsh, Jan, *Christina Rossetti - A Literary Biography*, London, 1994

Nunn, Pamela Gerrish, 'Rosa Brett, Pre-Raphaelite', *Burlington Magazine*, vol.126, October 1984

Peattie, Roger W. (ed.), *Selected Letters of William Michael Rossetti*, Pennsylvannia, 1990

Prettejohn, Elizabeth, *The Art of the Pre-Raphaelites*, London, 2000

Rossetti, William Michael, *Some Reminiscences*, 2 vols, London, 1906

Surtees, Virginia (ed.), *The Diaries of George Price Boyce*, Norwich, 1980

Thomas, Brian, *A Monkey among Crocodiles: the life, loves and lawsuits of Mrs Georgina Weldon*, London, 2000

6: Exhibition Catalogues

Casteras, Susan P. and Parkinson, Ronald (eds), *Richard Redgrave*, Victoria & Albert Museum, London, 1988

Gordon, Susan Phelps and Gully, Anthony Lucy, *John Ruskin and the Victorian Eye*, Phoenix Art Museum, Phoenix, 1993

Hewison, Robert, Warrell, Ian, and Wildman, Stephen, *Ruskin, Turner and the Pre-Raphaelites*, Tate Gallery, London, 2000

Sumner, Ann, *Ruskin and the English Watercolour: From Turner to the Pre-Raphaelites*, Whitworth Art Gallery, Manchester, 1989

Lenders

Aberdeen Art Gallery and Museums

Mr & Mrs David Barrie

Birmingham Museums & Art Gallery

Charles Brett

Family Collections

The Forbes Magazine Collection, New York

Gavin Graham Gallery

Christopher Gridley

Mary Horsfield

National Maritime Museum

National Museums & Galleries of Wales

Private Collections

Mr & Mrs Alfred Rankin, Jr

Sunderland Museum & Winter Gardens

Williamson Art Gallery & Museum, Birkenhead, Wirral (long-term loan
from Private Collection)

Patricia Smith

Tate, London

Jack Watson

Gillian Watson

Peter Watson